There Are Other Rivers

On Foot Across India

Alastair Humphreys

"For I have discovered that there are other rivers. And this my boys will not know for a long time nor can they be told. A great many never come to know that there are other rivers." ~ John Steinbeck

For Lucy

"Maatraan thottathu malligaikku manam irukkum."
"The far-off jasmine flower smells sweeter."

Author's Note

First of all, here's what this book is *not*:
- A book about India.
- A chronological account of a coast-to-coast walk across southern India.
- An epic adventure tale.

So what is it? Primarily this book is an attempt to articulate my fascination with the open road and the magnetism of the next horizon. I hope it will strike a chord with anyone restless and yearning for a long journey. I wrote it because I spend much of my time on big trips asking myself why on Earth I am doing it. And the answer is often not particularly clear.

The days are hot, hard and repetitive. I am often lonely, thirsty and tired. Yet I keep coming back for more. What is the enduring appeal of these days that have forged my adult life? They have made me who I am, both the bad and the good. These days have created most of my strongest memories and all my best anecdotes. These are the days of clarity that I turn to when I'm looking for answers and direction in my life. And I think to myself, "one day, on the road..."

I also wanted to try to share what a day on the road is actually like. So this is a tale about a single day on my walk through India, told by an idiot, full of sound and fury. I wanted to describe any day on the road, from any journey like this. It could have taken place anywhere, at any time since people began taking on these questing adventures. This is why I have removed all dates, time frames and names. Everything in this book is true. I have only re-ordered the incidents to build up my "day". It's a bit like Morecambe and Wise. They defended their terrible piano playing by saying they had "all the right notes, although not necessarily in the right order."

Most travel and adventure writing focuses on the occasional extraordinary stuff that happens amongst all the humdrum ordinariness. By definition, these incidents are not how most of the time on the journey is spent. The greatest expeditions in history are nothing more than a string of single days, most of them pretty uncomfortable and mundane. Perhaps long adventures are about nothing more than mining for the extraordinary? I don't think so. The average day on the road, the hundreds and thousands of normal days that make up the majority of my adventures, has a magnetism that draws me back time and time again. The terrible food, the sore feet, the repetitive conversations, the fungal rashes and the pummelling heat. The happiest days of my life. Any day, any journey. One day on the road.

There are many reasons why I chose to self-publish *There Are Other Rivers*. It may be interesting to share some of them here. I self-published my first book. I didn't do it through choice. I did it because no agents or publishers were interested in my story about cycling round the world. Trying to get my self-published book stocked in bookshops on a meaningful scale was futile and frustrating. Eventually though I found a publisher and began selling books in the traditional way. I will continue to do this where I deem it appropriate.

Fast-forward five years and five books and I am choosing to return to self-publishing. Why?

I love bookshops but they account for a tiny percentage of my book sales. Almost all my sales are online or at my talks. This book will not be for sale in any bookshops. What I lose by that I make up with the freedom I gain. Self-publishing gives me total control. I can share the story however I want. This is a linear, chronological journey but I wanted to share it in a non-linear way. That might not be sensible. It probably won't appeal to a mainstream audience. It may not even be a good idea. But it was *my* idea and I am willing to stand by it. I have produced this book as a Foldedsheet "mappazine" (which I really like), as a book of photography, a Kindle version, a PDF download, an audio book and even as a good old fashioned "normal" book. The schedule for getting all of this work done was determined solely by how hard I chose to work, how much coffee I drank and how little sleep I could survive on.

I wrote this book myself. I edited it and proof red it two. I will do all of the sales and marketing on my own. I acknowledge that the book would definitely have been better with the help of an editor, a proofreader and well-chosen test readers. But my walk through India was alone. I accepted that out there I would stand or fall by myself. This project is the same. It is risky. It is a bit stupid. But there are no excuses to hide behind and I like that. Self-publishing is an opportunity for simplicity, hard work and personal responsibility. Exactly like the journey I am writing about.

Another important aspect of self-publishing is that it can provide value for money, cutting out all sorts of middle men. I have priced all the versions of *There Are Other Rivers* as reasonably as possible. I am aware that this is only a short story and that I am not Shakespeare. But I hope that you feel it is value for money. Get in touch if you don't and I will send you a refund.

The internet makes self-publishing so simple. This returns a degree of power to normal people. I can never compete for the publishers' penny against celebrity travel authors or people who have had their trips on the telly and then dashed off a hasty book. Self-publishing gives a voice to people who have an interesting story, though perhaps one that will only appeal to a small niche. I am not a famous author hidden away behind PA's and PR teams. Send me an email or get in touch on Twitter. Tell me what you think of the book. I'll reply in person.

On the subject of the internet and social media, one of the hardest parts of self-publishing is informing a wide audience about the book. I would be extremely grateful if you could help spread the word about *There Are Other Rivers*: tell your friends or mention it online. Most helpful of all would be if you were willing to leave a quick rating and review on Amazon (www.tiny. cc/amazon_book_review) for this or any of my other books. I'm not looking for fake feedback – leave your honest opinion! If you already have an Amazon account this will take you less than a minute.

I hope you enjoy *There Are Other Rivers*.

Thank you!

Alastair Humphreys

England, November 2011

INTRODUCTION

"Beginning has the pleasure of a great stretching yawn; it flashes in the brain and the whole world glows outside your eyes."

"Beep... beepbeepbeepbeep... BEEPBEEPBEEPBEEP."

The alarm clock has just taken me on a journey. A journey that passed in an instant but which took me from one world to another. A journey from the magical world of dreams to a completely different one. A new world. A new day. India.

Why am I in India?

It does not matter that I am in India. This could be anywhere. Anywhere new to me. The story would be the same. What matters to me is *why* I am here.

—————

As soon as I hear the alarm I know where I am. I did not sleep well. I woke often, wondering if it was nearly morning, nearly time to begin. The coarse mesh of the mosquito net flopped against my skin, disturbing me. Mosquitoes whined and probed for my blood.

—————

I had been living in England, stationary, since my return from four years roaming the globe. I had crossed continents by bicycle and sailed across oceans. Now I had a home and I had a wife. I had settled down. Life was good. But perhaps that was the problem.

It began on the flight to our honeymoon. By the vagaries of the Great Circle, we flew over the colossal white emptiness of the Arctic. Far beneath us were huge sheets of ice, shattered like glass with thin leads of black water between them. I ate my peanuts and stared down. Guiltily I realised that, as much as sharing beaches and piña coladas with little umbrellas and my radiant bride, what I craved was the pain and hardship of a difficulty journey. I wanted insecurity, strife and what others want nothing to do with1. This had been missing since I settled down to my lovely life.

―――

Outside is dark. The sky presses black against the window. The street clamour that continued late into the night has now quietened. A brief pause before the melee of India wakes and begins all over again. I lie sweating on top of my sleeping bag liner, spread over the dirty bed. My head rests on a thin pillow. Untold numbers of bus drivers, pilgrims, travelling salesmen and minor bureaucrats have lain their heads here since its last clean. For a few seconds I absorb the last traces of sleep and steel myself for the day to come. Then I reach out and silence the alarm.

―――

---

1 This line comes from a poem I carried with me when I cycled round the world, *A Paratrooper's Prayer*: http://bit.ly/qHdbKZ. The other one I carried reminded me the struggles would become moods of future joys: http://bit.ly/rfCIII

I was in thoughtful mood as the plane landed. A friend of mine is a polar explorer. He was planning an expedition to the South Pole. I sent him a text message from the sunshine. I asked whether there might be room for two. (Did this count as marital infidelity, I wondered?)

I untangle myself from the mosquito net and stand on the concrete floor. I feel for the light switch. A pretty burst of blue sparks flash, the light flickers a few times then pings into life. Cockroaches speed to dark corners.

The walls are covered with smears, stains and scuffs. I don't care. It's just the usual squalid, cheap room. I slide my feet into flip-flops and shuffle to the toilet. Years of experience mean that instinctively I breathe only through my mouth as a precaution against the stink of Developing World toilets. I pee into a hole in the ground, scoop a jug of water from the bucket on the floor and pour it down the hole.

Ben replied to my text message.

"Yes."

I quit the second sensible job I had held in a year and, happily, abandoned my attempt at Real Life.

I was back doing what I loved and what I was good at. That is a good place to be. Arduous expeditions in the world's wild places. But now I was going to do it seriously. I was going to attempt to make a career from it. I began to earn enough money to get by, speaking and writing about my experiences.

Ben and I worked hard. We had the capabilities to succeed.

But financial meltdown had burst across the world. Unable to secure a sponsor we were forced to postpone the expedition for a year.

With the postponement came a window in the calendar for Ben to scratch an itch: an attempt on the solo North Pole speed record. I didn't begrudge that. But it meant that work stopped on our joint expedition whilst Ben's attention turned north.

I decided to do something interesting too.

I dump a scoop of water over my head. Its coolness jolts me. I pour a few more jugfuls, savouring the day's one moment of fresh cleanliness. I'm bracing myself for the day ahead.

Where should I go? And what should I do once I got there? India was a glaring omission on my Travelling CV. So India it was. For all the reasons vagabonds and wanderers have always gone to India. And because I had never been.

It never occurred to me to do anything other than a tough, cheap journey. Push myself hard. Try to achieve something that surprised me. These fundamental principles of my wanderlust have worn into my psyche since my first travels, like chariot wheels on a cobbled road, until I have come to accept them as permanent features of who I am.

I had enjoyed the freedom of travelling by bike, the minimalism, the outdoor life and the difficulty of it. I liked the way its slowness encouraged me to use all my senses. I loved the spontaneous adventures, opportunities and encounters it threw up. Anything less from this trip would be like looking out at the world through a thick dusty window, a trip round the harbour in a glass-bottomed boat after swimming with dolphins. Having cycled round the world I knew that another bike trip would be a step down, a feeble attempt to recreate a memory. So cycling was out.

I considered some of the things I enjoyed about cycling: the slowness, the simplicity, the physically arduous rhythm of the days. I extrapolated these on to their logical conclusion. How could I do something even slower, simpler and more miserable than cycling? Slow. Simple. Miserable...

I would walk.

The last piece of the jigsaw was where to walk. I liked the simple idea of walking from one coast to the other. I appreciate clear expeditions that can be explained fully in a sentence or two. Better still if they can actually be planned in a sentence or two[2]. I also fancied following a river, preferably a river with history and mystery and colour. Every river is taking a journey, one it has been on day and night for thousands and thousands of years. I find that fascinating. Pick any river on the planet and you will find an interesting journey.

I didn't have enough time to walk right across the top of India. So I guessed how far I could walk in the time available then worked south on a map until I found the latitude that corresponded with that distance. And then I went and did it. My trip was not far removed from grabbing a map, closing my eyes, jabbing my finger and going wherever it decreed. That's the way to have an adventure. Better still: grab a *globe*, spin, point, *go*!

---

2 Expedition aim: Walk across southern India, from coast to coast.
Expedition plan: Fly to India and take bus to the beach. Follow river on foot to its source then continue to the coast. Go home.

It mattered little where I went. The important thing was just to go. The downside of this approach was that I did not see the Taj Mahal, nor all the other metaphorical Taj Mahals that India is blessed with. I'd love to see them one day. But on this trip I just wanted to experience normal India. Normal people, doing their normal things in normal landscapes. Normal people with dignity and self-respect. I didn't want guidebooks telling me what to see, what to think and how many coins to hand down from my air-conditioned tour coach to the grubby hands of cute little poor kids. I wanted to get deeper than that.

I look at my reflection in the small plastic mirror hanging from a nail. I pass my hand across my scalp. A spray of water rises from the cropped stubble. Number 2 all over. It feels strange. I look strange, different.

My wife cut my hair the evening before I flew to India. She did it to humour me, for she thinks I look daft as a skinhead. I agree with her but I still like it. Shaving my head is a tradition at the start of my adventures. She ran the clippers and her soft hands over my head. My hair and 'Normal Me' fell to the floor around our feet in our London flat. Cutting my hair is partly pragmatic and partly symbolic. It's about leaving things behind. It's a new start. It's a simple indicator, as the hair begins to grow back, of how long I have been on the road. It's a reminder that I am going away to simplify things. Going where vanity and fashion are irrelevant and only personal performance is important. And it is a demand to myself to toughen up again and to stop taking myself too seriously.

Some friends had lived in India for years. They invited me for home-cooked Indian food and to discuss ideas for my trip. They also invited a couple who had lived and travelled in India for two decades. I took off my coat and was handed a frothing bottle of Cobra beer.

I felt that this evening would be crucial in determining whether my idea to walk across India had a future.

I walk back into the bedroom, the air cool on my wet body. Goosebumps rise on my arms. From the cold, I presume, though I am also anxious now about the day ahead. It's the nervousness of stepping out into the unfamiliar with no knowledge of what the day may bring.

It's time to get a move on.

The early signs were not encouraging. I looked down at the bubbles in my beer. I had just described my plans to the room in their entire detail.

"I want to, er, walk, er, from one coast of India to, er, the other. And maybe follow a river."

That was it.

This incisive briefing did not catalyse spontaneous applause, tossing of garlands, dabbing of tears or a standing ovation. Instead there was silence. Only a short silence, but one that was mere moments away from becoming embarrassing.

That was why I was staring at my bubbles with such interest. I was considering reaching for the peanuts, a classic manoeuvre for awkward moments. But I resisted showing weakness and decided to tough it out.

It was left to my fellow guest, the India expert, to break the silence. He was sitting in a leather armchair beneath a wall of books. He leaned forward with an uneasy expression on his face.

"I think," he stammered, "I think it might be a bit hot?"

It was a kind remark. Of all the flaws and follies and ignorance he could have exposed, he had begun mildly.

"Er, I don't mind the heat." I padded back.

"Where will you sleep? The decent hotels will be spread too far apart."

I sensed he was getting into his stride. His wife was looking at me with pity on her face.

Answering that I didn't really mind where I slept and that I would probably just hide behind some trees somewhere did little to reassure the concerned couple. Thoughts began tumbling from their mouths faster than they could turn them into sentences.

"What route will you take..? There are no decent maps..."

"Ah, I've bought a good map." I countered.

"The Eicher one is it?"

"Yes!" I crowed, relieved at last to have done something right.

"Thought so. Bloody useless."

By the time the food was ready we were all grateful for a change of conversation. My plan seemed like a disaster. But, unbeknownst to the others, I had been offered hope. It was just a throwaway remark, but I clung to it.

"If you are looking for a river maybe you should look at one of the seven sacred rivers. That could be fascinating..."

Could this be what I was looking for? This was not the time to pursue it. But I knew just the moment.

My movements are swift and precise, reduced over years of practice to a Zen-like minimum. The process of packing my life away and moving it on to the next unknown location down the road. I stuff the mosquito net and silk sleeping bag liner into the bottom of my rucksack. My flip-flops, diary and book go in the top. Toothbrush and toothpaste into a side pouch. Everything has its place. I fill my two water bottles from the bucket. Into each I squeeze three drops of dark brown iodine tincture. The iodine spirals and swirls beautifully, like ink, as it drifts down through the water, making it safe to drink. I screw the tops back on the bottles, shake them and place them in pouches on the rucksack's waistband.

Finally it is time to get dressed. I always leave this as late as I can, for after this the sweating begins. I sit on the bed. There is no bounce or give. I pull on my trousers, old nostalgic favourites from my bike trip. They are ripped on the right thigh, repaired raggedly, patched with a bruise of purple cloth.

I put on my shirt, the kind that looks smart in city offices. Except that this one is a couple of years past its best and much too big. I bought it in a charity shop last week. I can have the sleeves down to protect me from the sun or, like now, rolled up to the elbows. Same with the collar: it can be up or down and the front buttons can be open or done up. I use the breast pocket for the day's small change and my sunglasses.

I pull a money belt over my head. It sits round my waist, hidden beneath my shirt. It contains my passport, cash and camera memory cards. I'd hand over my pack to a robber without too much fuss, but I will run and I will fight for those memory cards.

I pull on brand new, clean-smelling socks. They won't be like this for long. I run my hands over my feet, making sure there are no creased seams that will rub. Finally I slip my feet into a pair of running shoes. I'm dressed. I wear the same outfit every day.

———

After good food, a few glasses of beer and lively conversation everyone was in good spirits. We helped clear the plates, piling them beside the sink. Then we ate fruit salad, light and refreshing after the curry. This was my moment.

A man I once knew taught me that decisive discussions are best held over dessert. He taught me much else besides. I think of that man often and I think of him again now. My life has changed a great deal since I knew him.

Casually I threw an open question to the table.

"So, you mentioned seven holy rivers..?"

Dinner had eased people's stance to my idea. Now they spoke more enthusiastically. They told of a river in southern India. A holy river, they said. A goddess. She flowed through temple towns and fertile farmland, a lifeline to millions. Neighbouring states squabbled over her waters. Home to crocodiles and elephants, she rose in the coffee-growing hills close to the west coast of India. The river flowed east, through forests shrill with birdlife, down to the hot lowlands. I tingled at the prospect of turning these tales, these imagined snapshots, into stories and memories of my own.

I was excited as I cycled home through the cold London night. The negativity of the evening had not worried me. I was used to it. I expected it and had long since learned to shrug it off and even feed on it. I was excited because I had found my river. Before I went to bed I quickly scribbled the river's name on a scrap of paper, in case I should wake in the morning and, like a dream, forget it.

I did not learn much more. I did not want to know about where I was going. I wanted to discover as I went along, about the river, India and myself. I wanted to test my nerve and my ability to survive and thrive anywhere in the world. I did not want the crutch of prior knowledge and the baggage of preconceptions added to all the stuff in my pack.

I booked a flight, the dates based purely on Ben's North Pole schedule. I made no calculations on how far or fast I would have to walk. I would do that on the way and push myself as hard as necessary to get it done in time. I didn't know if there would be villages along the way to buy food. But I knew I could carry supplies to last for many days and that water should always be available from the river. I was quite happy to sleep wild. I didn't need to know more. I did not care one bit where I was going or what I would find. I cared only that I was going. That was enough. Adventures like this require no real planning, no specialist gear or skills, nor even much money. All they demand is a big idea and the boldness to begin.

I am nervous now. I unpeel two of the tiny, sweet local bananas. Munch, munch and they're gone. I slip two more into my pocket to eat as I walk. It's time to go. I stand and lift the pack onto my back. It doesn't feel heavy. I bob up and down, shrugging the straps into place.

I pull back the bolt on the door. There is no more delay. I walk out of the room. The door clicks closed behind me. I've left comfortable familiarity behind. It's time to answer the call, to cross the threshold and to begin another day on the road.

The Walk

"You can boast about anything if it's all you have.
Maybe the less you have, the more you are
required to boast."

This book is not a chronological narrative about walking across India. I did that as I went, sharing my experiences through Twitter. It's like adventure haiku and a few excerpts should suffice to recount the walk.

> I've arrived in the glorious madhouse of India. Excited and daunted about beginning the walk.

> Munched by mosquitoes, sweating a lot and a bit overwhelmed. Tomorrow morning I begin.

> Ridiculously hot. Dreaming of lovely fresh mornings on my way to the South Pole.

> Played village cricket. Maintained England's reputation: caught in the deep for 0.

> Passed an elephant on the road today!

> I now have a stick for whacking evil dogs.

> Think I was guilty of underestimating this trip...

> Sleeping in a rice field tonight. Rice for dinner.

> A moon shadow, bats and the stars: a peaceful side to India at last.

> 300km down and no blisters – yet.

> BEEP! BEEP! Indian drivers driving me mad.

> Slept in a temple. Coracle fishermen at dawn.

> Hand washed my clothes. How long after returning home before loading the washing machine becomes a hassle again..?

> Policeman told me I was beautiful. I replied, "No, Sir, it is you who is beautiful." He liked that! Different to conversations with UK police...

> First blister.

> Filling a popped blister with iodine hurts a disproportional amount.

> Water crisis until teenagers drove 20km to fetch some for me.

> In an internet cafe using Google Maps to plot a route into the mountains: easily the best map of India I have found.

> Spent last night with a lovely family. Best curry yet. Thank you for your kindness!

> Watching policeman try to control traffic. Chaos! Too many chiefs..?

> I'm getting old and soft: the weight saving gained by cutting my toothbrush in half is now outweighed by its irritation factor.

> Enjoyed watching cricket on TV at the tea stand this evening: Pietersen (Bangalore) v Flintoff (Chennai).

> Beautiful hiking today, climbing up through coffee plantations. On foot beautiful usually = hard though. Tired.

> The road is behind me. The beach is empty and white past the palm trees. Ahead, only the sea. I can walk no further. The sun sets. The End.

@al_humphreys
#ThereAreOtherRivers

DAWN

"It was a morning like other mornings and yet perfect among mornings."

I walk quietly past the night watchman, bundled in blankets and snoring on the floor. I step out of the lodge. I'm out into the world. I have begun. Dawn will come quickly. But not yet. My pack feels comfortable. It's as small as I could manage, but we can't travel without baggage. We carry it wherever we go, even when we're trying to leave it all behind.

I glance up at the dark sky. I find Venus and use the bright star to check my bearings. I turn my back on it and begin walking west. I now know which direction I am going. That is virtually all I know about today.

One of the few certainties is the blazing heat and the noisiest country on Earth. So I breathe in the cool air and savour the silence while it lasts. Dawn smells different far from home. The air is full of possibilities. That's rubbish, of course. Air is air. Nothing more. But I'm excited to be on my way and am sniffing possibility all around me.

My legs are strong. My feet are comfortable. I have a sense of purpose. I'm here to learn and think and experience. And also to walk well and cover distance. To test myself. I feel good. I love it out here. The day has not yet knocked that out of me.

The street sweepers are already working. Bent double with one arm behind their backs, they sweep the street with short broomsticks made of twigs. They sweep, sweep, sweep at the dust, coconut husks, scraps of newspapers, cigarette ends and plastic bags. Sweeping India clean. Oxymoron, impossibility. Sweep, sweep, sweep. Sisyphus meets Escher. Sweep, sweep, sweep. Repeat day after day. Year after year.

With rhythmical arcs they sweep yesterday's unwanted remains into small piles. Perhaps an ox cart will collect them. Perhaps they will be rifled through by the stray dogs with sores and lame legs. Or perhaps their human rivals will beat them to it: India's unloved, nameless and destitute (who each, of course, have names and were, once at least, loved). They lie in doorways, their *lungis* (sarongs) wrapped tightly round their frail bodies like shrouds. They sleep the sweet hours of blessed escape when, if their dreams are kind, their lives are limited only by their imaginations. I wish them long sleeps. Is this the only kindness I can offer? Is this the best I can do?

I continue down the dark street. At dawn towns are quieter than villages. There are no cockerels, no bleating goats being led to pasture. I pass a small temple. The gate is still shut. On the outside wall is a small deity in a niche. A candle flame casts a tiny glow over the god. The wall above the statue is black with years of smoke. Rippling downwards is a red waterfall of solidified candle wax.

Dawn never arrives gradually. It comes in little leaps each time I notice that it has grown lighter since I last paid attention. The sky is greying. I can see further. I am past the shops and bus stand. There are homes beside the road now. Most are still dark but a few are beginning to stir. Through an open door I see smoky orange flames wrapping up around a cooking pot. A fat woman in a green sari stands sleepily in the doorway. She doesn't notice me.

The ground outside another home has already been swept and splashed with cow dung and water to keep the dust down. The fronts of India's rural homes are always pristine, even if just yards away a stinking pile of rubbish has been dumped. An elderly woman is marking out her *kolam* for the day. These elaborate, symmetrical patterns of white rice flour are redrawn each morning. They welcome guests to the home as well as Lakshmi, the beautiful four-armed goddess of prosperity. The old woman, bent double and concentrating on her *kolam*, does not notice either as I pad past. She pours white flour from her dark fingers in a thin, neat line, like sand rushing through an egg timer. Thousands of days have begun like this for her. I wonder how many remain.

Ahead of me a circle of light illuminates a cluster of men at a small tea stand. Two are sitting on a homemade bench. They are discussing the morning's newspaper, a broadsheet of few pages, inky photographs and swirling Indian script. The other men are standing, quietly sipping steaming glasses of milky tea. They hold them delicately at the rim as the glass is too hot to hold. Moths swirl round the bright bulb that hangs above the busy proprietor.

In a reminder to myself that this journey is about more than merely pushing through miles and pain, I stop. I enter the pool of light. I unclip my rucksack, roll it from my back and dump it on the floor. All eyes are on me. I stoop under the low thatched roof and sit on the end of the wooden bench. I look around, smile and blow out dramatically, suggesting that I am tired. It's not true: I've only walked a few miles. It's just a role I play. The road has taught me that this is an approach that works. It starts a conversation.

"*Chai?*" someone asks.

"*Chai,*" I agree.

It's time for a cup of tea.

FLABBINESS

*"You know how advice is: you only want it if it agrees
with what you wanted to do anyways."*

There are three stages of flabbiness in life. Each is more restricting
and stifling than the one before. They creep insidiously over me
like vines until it takes one hell of a struggle to escape their
clutches. If ever I feel the saggy symptoms snuffling up on my
life then I know it is time to hit the road.

The first stage of flabbiness, and the easiest to fix, is physical
flabbiness. It begins when busy schedules, dark winter days and
eating too much win the devil's footrace against the part of me
that knows that exercise isn't a waste of time but actually makes
me more efficient, alert and happy. Despite knowing this I am
still at times sufficiently idle to let my standards slip and my
fitness slide away. Fitness is like chasing a shoal of fish: difficult
to master and get on top of, easy to lose.

If I don't go running for a few days, I feel cooped up and ratty.
Leave it a few more and the habit is broken. I know I need to
run. I want to run. But I just can't be bothered. Flabbiness has
begun to set in, slowly, invasively, like cataracts. Before I know
it I am easing out my belt buckle and blaming my sloth on the
effects of age.

The second stage is mental flabbiness. Give up exercising,

33

stop forcing myself out the front door for a run and inevitably my mind starts to sag too. I used to feel alert and inquisitive. I read lots of books. But one evening I came home tired. Flopping down onto the sofa I reached for the television remote instead. Suddenly I am gripped by light entertainment. I realise how pleasant life can be if I stop thinking about it. It is much simpler to exist than to live. I've got a dishwasher and a coffee percolator and I drink at home most nights with the TV on. I sit slumped in front of the telly flicking round the channels until I have frittered away enough of my life that it's time to go to bed.

Finally, if I start forgetting any of these things, then I know I am on a slippery slope towards the third, terminal, stage of flabbiness: moral flabbiness!

- Each day I am one day closer to my death. No matter how aware I am of this, it is still sometimes difficult to believe in my own death.
- I don't know when I will die, so putting things off to an indeterminate date in an un-guaranteed future is pretty daft.
- I am happiest when I have a sense of purpose.
- There are so many places I would still like to see, so many interesting people to meet, so much to do. And there is so little time. Before I know it I'll be dead and what a bloody waste that will be if I've just been arsing around.

By the time I have succumbed to the debilitating onslaught of physical and mental flabbiness I am already well on the primrose path to moral flabbiness. Not only have I conceded my physical health and settled for candyfloss in place of a brain, I have accepted that this is good enough for my life. I have become comfortably numb. I have decided that *Friends* repeats and a Chinese takeaway are sufficient return for the privilege of being born, healthy and intelligent enough, in one of the richest, most free countries on the planet. I have a passport to explore the world. I will always be able to find some sort of work. I will never starve to death. It's hard really for me to come up with any decent excuses. The choice is all mine.

Life is too brief and too rich to tiptoe through half-heartedly, rather than galloping at it with whooping excitement and ambition. And so I explode in rage just in time. It's time to go prowling in the wilderness. It is time to live violently again. It is time to sort my life out. This can be done in two ways. I either jump in the nearest cold river for a bracing swim, or I plan a trip, set a start date and, come what may, begin.

Go

"The virus of restlessness begins to take possession of a wayward man, and the road away from here seems broad and straight and sweet."

An urge builds in me, a voice in one everlasting whisper, day and night repeated until I just have to go. It doesn't really matter where I go. All that matters is that I go. Somewhere different. Somewhere new. Maybe I get bored with where I am. Maybe the restless dissatisfaction rises from everything being too familiar, too easy. Whatever the cause, being in motion feels good.

It can be as simple as driving through the night, music playing, windows down, headlights picking out road signs and counting down the miles to new places. The moon sways back and forth overhead, mirroring the twists and turns of the road as I roll on under the stars. Turnings I don't take and pass with a pinprick of regret and curiosity. What would I discover down that road? Who would I meet? How would my life change? Places I will never see again, but it does not matter because I am on the way to even more that is new. It is the gleam of the untravelled world that drives me on. Go, go, go.

Before I begin a big trip nerves and excitement brew in my belly. I'm diffident by nature so the nerves generally outweigh the excitement. I worry about all that might go wrong and have to cajole myself instead to imagine the good things that might happen. I stir scenarios round and round inside my skull until they begin to drive me mad. I feel as though I am on a runaway train. But worse than that: it's a runaway train that I have set in motion myself. I can't jump off. My lazy streak gets to work, busily concocting reasons not to begin at all. Things are just fine here... Don't rock the boat...

It does not help when everyone I tell about my plans tries to persuade me to take a bus to the Taj Mahal instead.

"No, no, no," said a man on the beach at the very beginning of the walk. His face was serious, his head wobbling from side to side. "It is a Very Big River. You must enquire about the bus facilities instead. It is very barren. You won't even get a cup of water. Indian food is very spicy for you people. There is a very big valley. There are snakes. There is bamboo..."

Thankfully there is a tiny sliver of my brain that fights back. Without it I would never do anything interesting. It is a still, small voice that simply maintains that I must begin. I thank the man for his concern, assure him that I will definitely heed his advice and then do no such thing.

It is like a kayaker approaching a rapid. Once he reaches the point of no return he just has to go for it and trust himself to cope with whatever may be thrown at him. I am on my way. There is no point worrying anymore. I feel a surge of release and remember why I put myself through all these agonies. I love the thrill of beginning new projects. It is a feeling that makes me sing out loud and feel like the luckiest man alive.

River

"Don't you dare take the lazy way... Whatever you do,
it will be you who do."

I push through a bamboo grove to the river and sit beneath a teak tree. I write my diary and study my map, a computer print out of a survey from 1912. It's the best map I managed to find for this area. Having a river to follow provides a tangible, constant thread to the route. It automatically gives purpose and direction to the walk. My river is small and boisterous now. The contours are tight and curling. Earlier I passed a magnificent waterfall, the noisy blast an invigorating change from the usually sedate flow. Upstream from this wide, gentle bend is a red and white striped temple and a deep gorge jumbled with gigantic boulders. Cormorants dry their wings on the bank. Tucked amongst the tangled tree roots are small shrines to Shiva and flame-blackened statues of cobras.

There is a low babble of chatter from people bathing and washing clothes. A girl is singing. Old, paunched men with worn bodies are praying. They bathe then bow their heads. They lift their arms to the sky, muttering all the while. A beautiful young woman stoops to collect water. She strains to lift the full container. Shaped like an amphora it fits snugly into the curve of her hip and I watch the bones in her back ripple as she walks away.

This scene has played out, virtually unchanged, for centuries. It has taken place every day of my life without me ever being aware of it. India's enormity reminds me how small the sphere I live my normal life in is. It alters perspective. The ageless river reminds me that my own time is fleeting. This tableau will take place again tomorrow when I have walked out of it and on thousands of rivers that I will never see, right across India, on every day of my life.

I find myself wondering whether any other tourist has ever sat here before. I doubt it. I ask not as a member of the Lonely Planet generation boastfully ticking off experiences and trumping others' tales. I ask because I had wanted a journey far from the picture postcard views and picture postcard sellers. I wanted to feel that I was discovering places for myself rather than following a prescribed path. And I am delighted how easy that was to achieve. I am really enjoying my own slice of India. It is fresh, exotic and unfailingly fascinating.

My river has changed so much since I began walking. The meandering delta near the coast, its agricultural irrigation canals and religious bathing ponds (*kalyani*) feel a long way away now. I'm getting there. I look down at the water flowing in the direction I have come from and imagine how long it will take to flow all the way to the sea.

"Take your time," I urge the river. "Enjoy it. I did."

ROUTINE

"It's a hard thing to leave any deeply routine life, even if you hate it."

People looking at me walking through India might envisage my daily routine to be something like:
- Get up, walk.
- Lunch, walk.
- Eat, sleep.

There is more to it than that. Every day on the road includes many more tiny routines:
- Pack away everything I own each morning. There is a place for everything and everything goes in its place (unlike the messy chaos I live in at home).
- Find someone who seems intelligent to ask for directions. Check with someone else to make sure.
- Work out, across language barriers, from people who never walk, how far it is to the next source of drinking water.
- Establish, with no menus and no common language, what food is available.
- Eat food completely unlike what I was expecting.
- Study my map and calculate how far I have to go. Repeat at every rest break.

- Ask people if they will fill my water bottles.
- Think of new songs to sing.
- Wave/swear at beeping trucks and buses.
- Daydream about home or future trips.
- Answer the same questions for everyone I meet. "What is your good name? What is your native place? How many children do you have? What is your profession? How much do you earn? Why are you walking? Do you want a lift?"
- Dream of what I will eat when I get home (clue: it will not be curry).

Routine is comforting and reassuring. It is the backbone of any long journey or expedition. There is a point to everything I do. Do things well and the day and the journey improve. Do things shoddily and I pay the price.

Routine can be a curse as well as a crutch. After all, boring routine is what I ran from in the first place. And the grinding repetitiveness of the road's routine does wear me down on a long journey. I often ask myself how I managed four years of it on my bike. *Chapeau*, my young friend, *chapeau*.

At times then I need something different, a break from the routine. Something that makes all the grunt work worthwhile.

—————

I crest a hill and across the rain-freshened plain see a gleaming pavilion of shining gold. It is a monastery for exiled Tibetan monks. I stare in astonishment, having had no idea I would find this. My wild surmise is my reward for choosing to learn nothing about what lay along my route.

The Tibetans are mesmerising, dressed in their distinctive

scarlet robes. They feel like fellow foreigners after hundreds of miles of Indians. A gong sounds and young monks scuttle past, like schoolboys late for class, splashing through puddles. An elderly monk smiles at me from the broad double doors of the spectacular temple and beckons me inside. I leave my gigantic shoes amongst piles of small ones and walk barefoot into the temple.

Instantly I have to recompose my list of the highlights of this walk. The interior is a vast space. The walls are painted with myths and legend. Thick red pillars support the roof. Two birds fly through the cavernous space, their smallness helping me grasp how mighty the temple is. The crowning glories are three colossal, golden Buddhas that tower above us all. They shine even on this drab morning. Many hundreds of novice monks sit cross-legged on the floor, facing a huge central gong. Rows of candles burn and incense sweetens the air.

Not all the young monks are as awestruck as me. Some chat to their friends or fiddle with their long, rectangular boxes of holy texts. If they had mobile phones they wd hv bn txtIng.

After about ten minutes a tall monk crashes the gong. Hundreds of voices begin to chant. The sound is low and ragged at first. But the chorus grows stronger and stronger until it reverberates round the temple. I tingle with the power of simultaneous prayer from so many. I sit back and close my eyes. I try to imprint the sound deep into my brain so that I never forget this journey. I give thanks for the never-ending surprises of travel, the rewards earned by persistently climbing the grinding ladder of routine.

SUNRISE

*"And the world opened out. And a day was good to
awaken to. And there were no limits to anything. And
the people of the world were good and handsome.
And I was not afraid anymore."*

It is the *chai* stall's busiest hour of the day. The *chai* man is
bustling slickly through his well-practiced movements. The cup
of tea is a small part of his customers' day, but to him it is the
most important. The care he devotes to his task reflects that. It
seems a good strategy for a successful business. Start small, do
what you do with enthusiasm and do it very well. Stick to that
and growth will come.

He presides proudly over his small stall, dressed in a blue
lungi and yellow vest. His slender hands work gracefully,
methodically and quickly. He mixes the tea, sugar and boiled
milk flamboyantly, pouring it from one jug to another at arms'
length. With a smile he hands a glass of tea to each customer.

I do not linger long. There is a compromise between walking
far enough to finish the journey, balanced against slowing down
and savouring it all. My natural inclination is always to push out
more miles and make things harder on myself. As I thank the
owner and the customers who have made me welcome (*"nandri,
nandri, nandri"*), I notice that the sky is already growing lighter

behind me. I walk on.

These first hours of the day are my favourite. Coursing through me is the drug that fuels my journeys, the feeling that keeps me coming back for more, despite my long-held feeling that I am not ideal material for this life (too soft, too hasty, too introspective). It's a fresh morning. I am someplace new on the far side of the planet. I am lean and very fit. The road stretches enticingly ahead of me. My legs ask to be tested and I lengthen my stride, accelerating with the glow of well-being. I'm eager to tackle the miles ahead and intrigued by what the day will offer.

I follow a meandering little road through green sugarcane fields. The broad river, my river, is on the right, flowing slowly in the opposite direction to me. Enormous cotton wool clouds glow pink, lit from beneath the horizon by the sun. Men are already working in the fields, wielding sickles as their grandfathers' grandfathers would have done. Will their grandchildren do the same, I wonder?

A temple on the far bank looks fabulous in the honeyed light. Its pyramidal *gopura*[3] stands twenty metres tall, every inch carved with gods and legend. It is a scenic view, very National Geographic, until I look closely and notice people squatting and shitting alongside those brushing their teeth or collecting water. The world is awake now, though the day is still quiet. People who are up early move with a quiet purpose. I love this time of day. Before the crowds swell there is more world to go round, more magic to share amongst those of us who are awake.

On the river a fisherman casts his net from a coracle, as his grandfather's grandfathers would have done. The net lands gently and the reflections of those extraordinary clouds ripple across the smooth water. It is a mesmerising scene, unchanged

3 The monumental gateway tower at the entrance to Hindu temples.

in hundreds, perhaps thousands of years. The fisherman's mobile phone rings. I hear him jabbering away as he hauls in his net. Will his grandchildren also fish like him?

Though it is early, young boys are already playing in the river. They shout and splash around the washing *ghats*[4]. When the boys see me, they start showing off, spinning and twisting as they leap into the water. I take some photos then show the boys my shots. Showing people the image on the back of my digital camera causes amazement on this walk. For most, it is a complete surprise. They are wet and noisy as they jostle round me for a better view of the camera.

A man wearing a red *lungi* and a vest passes as he returns from his morning wash. He is holding a piece of soap and a chewing twig. He invites me, shyly, to photograph the flowers in his garden.

We walk away from the road towards a cluster of small homes set back amongst trees. The orange earth is packed hard and smooth. The homes are painted baby blue. There is a small hayrick outside each one. Many have a buffalo too, tied through the nose and chewing methodically. Fishing nets are draped to dry alongside swathes of colourful saris. A young girl in a blue school uniform is washing shiny metal trays at a water pump. Next to her is a mound of yellow bananas. Her face is smeared all over with green paste and a bright scarlet *bindi* dot beams from her forehead.

Kids dash forward to see me, curious, excited and a little scared. My new friend (like many in South India his name is a multi-syllabic tongue twister that I do not catch) is the centre of attention with me at his side. He went out to brush his teeth and returned with a pink Englishman. Everyone is calling to him,

4 Broad concrete steps found on the riverbank in every town and village.

laughing and questioning. He enjoys the fun and I don't mind it either. It is good-humoured. But this reaction to me plays out many times every day. It is an aspect I do not miss when I return home and become part of an anonymous majority once again.

The man is proud of his garden. He has planted a couple of rows of flowers, about ten in each row, in front of his home. He waters them from an old plastic bottle and then gestures for me to come, look, enjoy. It is humbling and inspiring to see something planted, purely for pleasure, by someone with little spare time or money.

The sun is rising now. It's not a spectacular one today, but all sunrises are good to see, if only for the smug feeling of knowing that nearly everyone else is asleep and missing this moment. I think how rarely I watch the sunrise since I settled down to life in England. I resolve to start rising early again when I return home. I make many resolutions when I'm on the road and dreaming of home. I think how I'll make a better fist of it next time and make plans for a better-lived future, but already I know that I will never stick to this one.

"Here comes the sun, little darling," I sing loudly, every day, at the moment the sunlight first strikes my face. "It's alright, it's alright..."

It's a road tradition begun thousands of mornings ago, thousands of miles from here, in the cold, oxygen-starved heights of the Andes. There the faintest hit of warmth was welcomed. This morning the sunrise is thick and warm, rich with oxygen and the sweet reeks of India. Of dust and petrol fumes, of curry and cows (of rice and men?), festering drains, flowers and a thousand kerosene cookers. There is no place I'd rather be. Bliss is it in this dawn to be alive, but to be on the road is very heaven.

ESCAPE

*"For it is said that humans are never satisfied, that
you give them one thing and they want something
more. And this is said in disparagement, whereas it
is one of the greatest talents the species has and one
that makes it superior to animals that are satisfied
with what they have."*

Head thumping heat shimmering sun beating. Loneliness in
crowds of foreign tongues staring at one foreign face. Bruised
feet dragging spirit bruised shoulders slumped. Can't think.
Can't speak. Just walk. The monotony of the open road.

These are common complaints on a difficult journey. I often get
them all in a single day, and know there will be more of the same
tomorrow. Most days involve very little *except* for this carousel of
discomfort. It doesn't sound like much of an escape.

Yet escape is a key part of the appeal of the road. All my adult
life I have felt the need to get away. Its intensity and frequency
ebbs and flows but it has never gone altogether. Perhaps it is
immaturity, perhaps a low tolerance threshold. But there is
something about rush hour on the London underground, tax
return forms and the spirit-sapping averageness of normal life
that weighs on my soul like a damp, drizzly November. It makes
me want to scream. Life is so much easier out on the road. And

so I run away for a while. I'm not proud of that. But the rush of freedom I feel each time I escape keeps me coming back for more. Trading it all in for Simplicity, Adventure, Endurance, Curiosity and Perspective. For my complicated love affair with the open road.

Escaping to the open road is not a solution to life's difficulties. It's not going to win the beautiful girl or stop the debt letters piling up on the doormat. (It will probably do the opposite.) It's just an escape. A pause button for real life. An escape portal to a life that feels real. Life is so much simpler out there.

But it is not only about running away. I am also escaping to attempt difficult things, to see what I am capable of. I don't see it as opting out of life. I'm opting in.

On this walk my feet and shoulders are the vital parts of my body. My face, my looks and my hairstyle are irrelevant. Out here nobody knows who I am. Nobody knows what I have done well in my life. Nobody knows what I have failed at. I'm just a guy on a walk[5].

———

I take a photograph of myself resting in a bus shelter. Only since returning have I figured out why I like it. It's a photo that captures my youth. The days and years alone on the road. The thousands of miles, defining my life. Thousands of brief rests in shaded bus shelters like this one. I know that I will never live days quite like those again. I am tired but smiling. My pack is by my side. I have had that pack for almost 20 years now. I'm wearing an old hat, a veteran of scores of countries, unrecognisable now as the

---

5 Walking across India does not mean I am perceived as a blank canvas. What do people see? A white man. A British man. A dirty man walking in the heat. Assumptions will always be made. But at least here they are novel.

cricket hat it began life as. I must be somewhere remote for it's rare to take a photo without a curious Indian face peering into the frame. It's a self-portrait: I am alone. Nobody else sees this moment. It's just me and my thoughts out on the road, where every new horizon is filled with promise.

SIMPLICITY

"Simplicity, simplicity, simplicity! We are happy in proportion to the things we can do without."

A couple of years ago I was out on the crumpled ice of the frozen Arctic Ocean. It was bitterly cold. And I was deliriously happy. It was the stark simplicity of life out on the ice that I enjoyed so much. I had very few things to focus on each day, but I had to do each one to the best of my ability. If I did not then the consequences in those conditions could be severe. I decided, as my hands and nose thawed out back in the tent, that when I become King of the World this would be a good decree to run the world by:

- Concentrate only on the stuff that really matters. Cut everything else.
- Do what you do to the very best of your ability. Do this every single day. Otherwise you die!

Walking across India was not a case of life or death. But it was a similarly refreshing draft of straightforwardness away from the noise and clutter of the 21st Century.

As I walk upstream towards my goal the river becomes smaller and smaller. There are fewer diluting, polluting branches or confusing tributaries. Slowly I am moving away from the broad, stagnant channels of the delta towards the single holy well at the source.

I wanted simplicity. Simplicity of purpose and to travel as light as possible. I wanted to pare life down to the basics again. India was a crash diet for me after the creeping lassitude of easy living.

Simplicity of possessions felt difficult to achieve, accustomed as I had become to life, liberty and the pursuit of stuff. Yet it is liberating and enriching. Carrying all my possessions through a hot Indian day is a sweaty penance for materialism. It helps me focus on what I need. What I *really* need. The clothes I stand up in, plus a spare pair of socks, a *lungi*, flip-flops and a clean shirt now feels ample. A wise man once said that the things you own end up owning you. On the road you have few owners. Thoreau got it right, wanting to "live deep and suck out all the marrow of life, to live so sturdily and Spartan-like as to put to rout all that was not life."

As I remove myself from needless material stuff, my mind also begins to unwind and I enjoy a lighter mental load too. I cleared my diary, turned off my phone and computer, and cleared off. I have de-cluttered my mind. I am wandering across a country, chatting to people, taking photos, making notes and drinking tea. By the standards of the real world, I am bumming around. I am not earning money, for heaven's sake! Isn't it time you got a *real* job, young man?

"Adventurer and Writer?" comments a bright woman with a sparkle in her eye as she reads my business card. "Some may say, Alastair, that you are actually a wastrel. A vagabond."

I disagree with her poetic description. I am filling my days with purpose, even if it is only a very simple purpose. That is not a waste.

Each day I have to walk as far as I can, as near to my river as possible. And I must find food and water and shelter. That is all. If I do just those few things then I have not wasted my day. Far from it. I have used my day fully. A day working hard on a project I care about is a day well spent. Find something you love. Do it well. Do it a lot.

It feels good to carry my world on my back. I smile in the sunlight. I could travel and live this lightly forever, I remember as I get into my stride.

ALONE

"All great and precious things are lonely."

Odd choice, India, if I wanted to be alone. But being alone is an important part of my journeys. Alone time. A lonely time. Alone with all of India. I feel more alone when I'm jostled by a billion strangers than somewhere wild and empty. But what is alone?

Alone might be out in the hot scrub, watched by nervous deer. The only sound inside my head is my heart thumping. Everything is motionless except for the crunch of a family of wild elephants walking slowly past. I stare, awestruck, as small as a world and as large as alone.

Or alone might be on the roof of a cheap guesthouse at sunset, having walked for hours through the crowds and chaos – like a murmuration of starlings – to reach the centre of the city and this brief moment of sanctuary. I watch the busy streets as parakeets dash madly for home, whooshing past in clusters. The call to prayer drifts lyrically across the city on the hot breeze. I feel a sense of exhilaration swelling inside me that howls,

"Woohoo! I can't believe I am here, in India, doing this. This is special. I am lucky."

I love this kick, the rush and buzz of joy and freedom. Just being in motion for the sheer heck of it. This is the unbeatable intensity of solitude that keeps me hooked on travelling alone.

I love the continual exposure to new people, new faces and new ideas. And I appreciate being forced to make my own decisions and accept their consequences. I have to trust myself, encourage myself and boss myself all at the same time. The effort, the responsibility and the opportunity are all mine.

Being alone forces me to be resilient and flexible. There can be no coasting, letting somebody else make the decisions, work out the route and find somewhere safe to sleep. And there are no ties, constraints or compromises. I can do what I want, go where I want, be who I want. It is an undeniably selfish pleasure.

I miss those I left behind. Being alone adds a lick of lonely melancholy to the lovely moments. I can never share these memories with anybody. But being alone also adds a sheen of silence to each sunset and moonrise; the greedy pleasure of having it all to myself. Nobody within thousands of miles knows who I am. Nobody knows my name. I can be intimidated by that or relish the freedom it offers.

SNAPSHOT

"The Earth teaches us more about ourselves than all the books in the world."

All the clichés about India are true. Clichés always are. But there is so much more. There always is. India: so vivid and loud. Energetic and mad. Charming, ingenious, squalid and callous. In my head I see all this. I suspect that anyone who has been to India and not just stayed in an International hotel will do too. But I fear that if you haven't been to India then I am going to fail you. I don't have the capacity to bottle the extraordinary essence of India. This is a pity as India is among my favourite of all countries, even though I have seen little of it.

My first impressions of India, like generations of travellers before me, were intense and conformed to stereotypes. The filth, the chaos, the poverty, the stupid driving. The bright saris, the delicious food, the instinctive, gentle civility.

After a few weeks on the road I'm settling in to India a little and getting used to how things work. I sit in the shade at a street stall drinking *chai*. The day feels oppressive. I eat. Dust. Noise. Glare. Stares. Music. Engines. Cell phones. Car horns. I need to hide from it all for a few minutes.

A lorry beeps *Silent Night* loudly as it reverses. Oh, the irony. There are grubby finger marks round doors and half-removed bill posters and election flyers on half-painted walls. There are crates of empty glass bottles awaiting collection and strips of shampoo sachets hanging above shop counters. Bicycles squeak by, daring to compete with the lunatic drivers. They all have old sprung saddles, rod brakes and a bell.

I flick through a newspaper, mostly reading the small articles and adverts. In the same way that I chose to walk an unglamorous slice of India, I prefer the small oddments of news rather than the main, attention-grabbing, Taj Mahal-esque headlines.

There have been surprise checks at various government offices to improve punctuality and attendance of staff. All officials were found to be absent from the Chemmedu Agriculture Extension Centre and Sericulture Department Office.

Health officials have been directed to take steps to appoint a driver for their ambulance.

An unknown, destitute old woman was mauled to death by stray dogs inside the grounds of the City Hospital.

Polling has been peaceful bar stray incidents of violence, rigging attempts and group clashes. A district general secretary was hacked to death.

A politician campaigns with the promise of free colour televisions for all. Asking a rally if they thought this was a good idea, he received "thunderous applause instantly."

I buy a glossy magazine, my curiosity piqued by the first hint of laddish culture I have seen in India. The magazine is expensive,

£1.50, almost as much as I pay for a night's lodging. I don't think I've yet met anyone who would spend so much on a magazine. It is simplistic and aspirational. Its wealthy, urbanite readers are playing at being Western. On the front cover is a pouting babe in bodice, knickers and suspenders. Articles in the magazine include "10 things we bet you didn't know about porn!" and "Drink smart: we tell you how."

I turn to the advice pages.

Question: "Should western commodes be kept open or shut when not in use? I've read stuff about women wanting the toilet seat down while men want it up or something like that? What's the right funda [sic]?"

Answer: "Western toilets should be kept shut. There is a lid, right? Use it!!"

Meanwhile an old television is playing in the shop behind me. It's showing a glamorous horse racing event heaving with beautiful, rich Indians trying to look European. This too is so far removed – several generations removed, I imagine – from what I have experienced in my narrow slice of India. I really hope that, as more and more people rise out of poverty, India does not just copy Western fads and trends.

Move just a few streets away from the centre and a town quickly feels more like a large village. Cowpat discs, to be used as fuel, dry outside homes painted with brand logos like Vodafone. Cows amble the streets, munching on rubbish. People gently and reverently touch the animals' flanks as they pass. Children play with homemade kites. This is a different world to the town centre and the television. They do things differently there. I accept the folly of trying to make generalisations about a billion people, from billionaires to beggars, scattered across thousands of miles.

MORNING

"And again there are mornings when ecstasy bubbles in the blood, and the stomach and chest are tight and electric with joy."

The water in the emerald paddy fields glints as I walk. A confetti of butterflies flutters in the air. The roadside palms are painted in black and white checks. I enter a village with music blaring from speakers rigged on bamboo poles. I always like places that play music out loud (it's quite common in parts of Eastern Europe, China and Latin America), even in the countries where it's done with Orwellian undertones.

This feels like a happy town, a happy morning, except, I guess, for the goat who is about to be butchered on the roadside. I stop to watch. The knife is sharp and swift and one elegant slice ends the goat. How fragile, life! So very easy to die. So final. Is this a beautiful, musical morning to die? Or so beautiful and musical that the thought of death feels too sad to bear?

The goat is dead. It lies in the dust. There is very little blood. The butcher works swiftly, turning the animal into joints of meat. His customers wait patiently. I am fascinated by the neat and tidy compartments of organs inside the goat that had, until moments before, been working magically well.

Morning on the road is about the satisfaction of committing to action. Of being in motion and not yet demoralised or tired. The nerves have passed. It's a positive time of day. Everything is still fresh. It is up to me to fill this day. I picture what I would be doing back home and what my friends might be doing right now. I'm glad to be out here (as opposed to later in the day when I'm longing for home and an easy life).

I am rarely without company. People always want to talk to me, to find out about this strange Englishman walking briefly through their lives. I walk from one identical conversation to the next. Why don't you take a bus? Do you know Freddy Flintoff? Every day I see children playing cricket in the fields, the pitch scratched out on a patch of flat earth. They are always delighted if I stop to join their game.

"England against India!" I declare as the boys squabble over who will bowl at me first.

I am still cheerful and energetic enough to greet everyone I pass. I always say "good morning" to children in English, as I know they have learned at least this much in school. They might as well put it into practise for the first, and perhaps only, time in their life. A conversation usually follows that is identical across the non-English-speaking world.

Me: "Good morning."

Child: "Good morning."

Me: "How are you?"

Child: "I am fine."

Me: "I am fine too. Goodbye."

Child: "Goodbye."

I walk on, followed by giggles and incredulous gasps.

I walk through a village where outside every home small piles of mangos are for sale. So many places in the world operate this way. One product per season. Harvest it, eat it, enjoy it, sell it. When it's gone, it's gone. Each town and region has their own speciality. These are places not yet homogenised (or diversified) by the efficient distribution networks we are accustomed to. At home I can eat strawberries all winter with no real feeling of appreciation or surprise. We have everything, all the time, which means also that we have nothing special. But here, now, walking into mango season, or mango region (I'm not sure which), I slurp with sticky satisfaction at this unexpected bonus to my day, munching mangos as I walk. I do not know how many villages I will walk through before I leave the mango behind. It's an ephemeral pleasure and all the sweeter for that.

I pause at a water pump and wash my hands and face. I clank the long metal handle and dunk my head beneath the gushing burst of water. The day's heat is beginning to build and I shiver at the delicious coldness of the water. The water runs down my face and neck, wetting my clothes. The sun will bake them dry again only too soon. I fill my broad-brimmed hat with water and up-end it on my head. I fill my bottles with enough water to get me to the next village and walk on.

Rooks caw and swirl above me. A funeral is taking place. The whole road from the home to the burial site, shaded beneath three gnarled trees, is strewn with yellow, orange and pink flowers.

"Funeral processions clatter
Down streets with drums and rose-petals,
Dancing death into deafness."

The task now is simple: blast out as many miles as I can manage before it gets too hot. I am earning my lunch break. The river teases me, tempting me to swim. But a combination of crocodiles, pollution and my impatient obsession with ticking off miles dissuades me. I snatch occasional respite in scraps of shade. After a few more hours I am beginning to suffer.

The first negative thoughts creep in. I miss home. I feel a hint of annoyance that every vehicle or moped beeps at me, even on these rural lanes. That every time I pause a cluster gathers to stare and snigger and ask the same questions I've been asked a million times before. I ask why I'm putting myself through this, a question I've asked myself a million times before.

It feels like a taking up of the strain, a satisfying stiffening of the challenge, like cranking up the treadmill pace a notch or two. The exercise in masochistic suffering has begun.

CURIOSITY

"I've never been content to pass a stone without looking under it. And it is a black disappointment to me that I can never see the far side of the moon."

Go somewhere new, try something different and life fizzes with questions. What will happen? How will my life change? How will I change my life?

No imagination has ever conjured up anything so unique, vivid and complex as any view on this planet. I am fascinated by what lies around the next corner. Like the lucky dip at a fairground, I was eager to delve into India, a country I had not been to, and rummage around in the sawdust with no idea what prizes I would pull out.

The Explorer, by Rudyard Kipling, tells of the lure of the unknown. The mountain ranges called to the explorer until he was drawn to find out what lay beyond them, even when people told him not to bother, that it was not possible. Curiosity took him "along the hostile mountains, where the hair-poised snowslide shivers" and through "the big fat marshes." The hero, paradoxically, is content not to be a hero. He lets others take the plaudits and the spoils from his accomplishments. What then was his reward, if we assume rewards to be necessary? Primarily, it was a satiation of his curiosity. It never made him rich but the explorer ends his journey with a sense of satisfaction.

I am also drawn by the randomness and unpredictability of horizon chasing. I like having to respond to new situations. Out here I do not just have the opportunity for spontaneity; I am compelled into living spontaneously. I often fear this in anticipation, but love it in hindsight.

I know that these are the fun times, the mad times, the exciting times. Living by my wits. Trusting them to keep me alive. Standing on a hilltop and singing at the sky with no idea where I will sleep tonight but with enough chutzpah to be confident that it will all work out and enough positivity and humour to accept that the worst thing likely to happen is a long uncomfortable night. Morning will come. The sun will rise. And I will sleep extra well tomorrow because of tonight's travails.

There is enough in this world for many lifetimes. But if the flavour of the ocean is contained in a droplet why can I not just be satisfied with all that is around me right now? Why am I constantly probing for something else? Is this the trait of an optimist or a pessimist? Am I always hoping for even better round the next corner? Am I just dissatisfied with the present, with my 'now'? Or am I somewhere in between? In purgatory, searing away the bad, the weak and the superfluous in the hope that I'll find a solution at last. The road rolls on and on. On towards the next horizon. It's the most enticing page-turner I've ever known. And all I have to do is walk on to try to find out if the far-off jasmine flower really does smell sweeter.

FOOD

*"What does a man need, really need? A few pounds
of food each day, heat and shelter, six feet to lie down
in and some form of working activity that will yield a
sense of accomplishment."*

A boy asks me about English food. I find it hard to describe,
particularly without mentioning the delicate subject of roast
beef.

"Is it burger? Pizza?"

And because it is hot I just agree with him.

Indian food is even harder to summarise. It is certainly very
different to the Great British Indian Takeaway. It is rarely
fluorescent orange. However, although there is undoubtedly a
vast variety of food across the whole of India, in any one place, at
any one time of the year, the poor people will eat a very limited
repertoire. Most places serve the same one or two dishes. I eat
them every day until a hundred miles or so later a new option
emerges. The general theme, however, is always "curry".

I eat curry for breakfast. I eat curry in the mid-day heat. I eat
it three times every day. And I eat a lot of rice. I eat rice served
on broad green banana leaves. I eat it in compartmentalised
tin *thali* trays. I even pour water over it, mush it up with my
hand and eat it that way. I eat *idli* (steamed rice cakes) and

69

dosa (crispy rice pancakes) and rice served with various sauces (*sambar*) and curd. I eat in places where the rice keeps coming until you are full. I eat in places where I am presented with a banana and a smile at the end. The charm is that I never know what I will get next. Everything surprises and amuses me.

—∞—

After eating curry every day for weeks I am sick of it. So one day, when I smell a different aroma, my taste buds explode. In greedy excitement I follow my nose to a stand where a boy is stirring a sizzling pan.

The smell of the spices is so different to what I am accustomed to.

Chilli, garlic, onions…

I am drooling and excited. It smells new and delicious.

Excited, I call out to the cook,

"What region is this food from?"

"China."

LEARNING

"And this I believe: that the free, exploring mind of the individual human is the most valuable thing in the world."

My life really got going the day I finished formal education. I began enjoying learning at about the same time, when I began wandering the world. Knowledge became gold dust. No longer was I learning stuff merely to regurgitate it in hot exam halls. I do appreciate the benefits of the little bits of paper I earned, but school on the road is different. Geography, culture, history, politics, religion: the way of the world begins to fit together. And the more I learn the more I learn how little I know.

Travel far from home and even mundane, ordinary events become out of the ordinary and fascinating. Knowledge and exciting fresh perspectives are thrown at me all the time. This doesn't happen when life's normal routine is ticking over. But I do have to caution myself to travel slowly. If I rush my journeys, one eye on the clock, eager only to tick off miles, countries or sights, then I'll accumulate lists, but I won't learn much. Truman Capote would dismiss it out of hand: "that's not travelling, that's moving."

But backpackers and other holiday makers will learn at least as much about India as I will on my walk. And I hadn't even particularly cared whether I did this walk in India or any other place on the planet. So I am not really doing this to learn specifically about India. What I want to learn from this experience, spending time amongst lives very different to mine, is about myself and the direction of my life. The slowness of a walk is a good chance to reflect on the past and contemplate the future, two things I never get round to doing at home. I am yet to find a better recipe for really learning about myself than a physically difficult, uncomfortable adventure thousands of miles from home.

LANDSCAPE

*"And then – the glory – so that a cricket song
sweetens his ears, the smell of the earth rises
chanting to his nose, and dappling light under a tree
blesses his eyes. Then a man pours outward, a torrent
of him, and yet he is not diminished. And I guess a
man's importance in the world can be measured by
the quality and number of his glories."*

Most adventures revolve around beautiful landscapes and impressive wildness. But not this trip. This project was about normal-ness. I was not seeking the Top Ten Tourist Views of India. I did not see the Taj Mahal. I was looking for ordinary India (what an oxymoron!). I didn't want the tourist highlights because I didn't want the hassle, expense, disappointment and tedium that accompany them. And I wanted to see things I had never seen before, not even in a photograph. I wanted to see what real India was like, in the same way that a visitor to Britain will learn little from taking a photograph of Big Ben.

At walking pace, there are always interesting landscapes. Being outside all day and often all night as well, I tune in to the rhythms of nature. I wake at dawn and sleep at nightfall. I know where and when the moon will rise. I notice if the wind changes direction or if clouds begin to build in the sky. There are places of beauty, such as the beach where I begin the journey. I walk along the hot white sand, followed by dark-skinned children with huge white eyes and smiles. Pulled up to the high tide line is a row of narrow wooden fishing boats, pirogues. It feels wonderfully far from London. Waves roll gently up the sand and the air smells of sea salt. It is a fine place to begin a journey. Unusually for me, I do not stare out at the ocean and want to cross it to see what is on the other side. All my thoughts are inland, along the route of the river I am about to follow.

I run my hands through the warm river water as it mingles with the sea. This is a pilgrimage site for Hindus. A father mutters prayers and dunks his shining, surprised-looking baby several times beneath the water. A dozen men sit cross-legged in prayer round a small fire. Each has a coconut, broken open as an offering, *puja*. I breathe in the sea air, look forward to the next time I smell it, and begin to walk.

Hundreds of miles later, after walking towards the sunset each day, I have left the hot plains behind. The riverbank is tangled with trees and boulders and the tiny road struggles to hug the river valley. It climbs high and drops down, twisting round the compass, through forested hills. Coffee estates are dotted on hilltops, the coffee planted in amongst the tall forests. Birds screech and cicadas click feverishly. They fall silent until I have passed. I love the aroma of fresh cardamom, the hum of beehives and the creeper-hung trees dripping with moisture. Not a bad landscape to walk through, I think happily. Not bad for a haphazardly chosen strip of India unheralded in the Sunday papers' Best of India pullouts.

Joy

"Every man has a retirement picture in which he does those things he never had time to do – makes the journeys, reads the neglected books he always pretended to have read."

I like doing exciting, unusual things, particularly if they are thousands of miles from home and laced with an element of risk. The call to adventure is hard to ignore. And life is not all work. It's not all Nietzsche and granola, penance and planning for retirement.

"I won't have it," declared Annie Dillard. "The world is wilder than that in all directions, more dangerous and bitter, more extravagant and bright. We are making hay when we should be making whoopee."

I want fun and joy and laughter in my life. Many people dream of travelling the world when they retire or win the lottery. My trip is inspired by similar motives to people who sign up for the retirement cruise of a lifetime. It is just a lot cheaper than a cruise. Walking across India cost £500, of which £300 was the plane ticket. I want good food and the warm glow of the sun on my face. I want to visit beautiful places, see shooting stars on warm evenings and forget about life for a while. These are the joyful times. The good times.

There is nothing complicated to this: travelling the world and living adventurously is a lot of fun. When people ask, "why do you do this?" there is no simpler or more honest answer.

PEOPLE

*"I wonder how many people I've looked at all my life
and never seen."*

The people I meet are a highlight of the journey. I meet good
people, kind people, funny people, mad and sad and one or two
bad people. But mostly it is a random selection of good people.
Many invite me to their homes for *chai*, for food or to spend
the night.

One day a stylish man stops his motorbike to chat for a few
minutes. His hair is swept back, he has a big bushy beard and
a smear of red paste on his forehead. He wears three gold rings
and a chunky gold necklace. His pretty wife and daughter are
perched on the back. They are sharing the headphones of an iPod
Shuffle. He works in a bank. He hands me his business card.

"Come and drink tea when you reach my town!" he calls as
the family hoot, wave and roar away.

I take up the invitation. The bank is the first air-conditioned
building I have been into in India. I am aware of how dirty I
am. I find my new friend at a computer, data-entering a pile
of cheques. My shoes stink. He smiles in welcome, shakes my
hand and slaps me on the shoulder.

"Let us drink tea."

I want to ask some of the questions I've been unable to answer walking through areas where nobody spoke much English. About rural poverty and India's rising power, about the caste system, inequality and water wars. But he is not interested in any of that. He only wants to know about England. It's good to be reminded that my normal life, my normal home and normal country are as interesting as anywhere else when seen with fresh and open eyes. The barrage of questions is charmingly frank.

"Are you having love marriages or arranged marriages? If your father does not like your girl will he ban you from his home? Are you circumcised? How many castes are there in England? Are you Christian? Are English villages like Indian villages? Do villages have water and electricity as well as the towns? Does it really rain everyday?"

I still have not seen an angry person. Indians seem to share the same mild characteristics as their revered cows. But one day I see an Indian cry. The sight jolts me. A middle-aged man, his spectacles askew, a friend's arm round his shoulder, pushes through the market crowd. His eyes are shiny and numb with grief. Surrounded by the noise and rush of so many strangers it is easy to forget that each has an individual story.

Most of my memories of people are from the briefest of connections. Moments that flash through the gulfs between our lives and simply connect on a human level. A woman, about my age, is running down the road towards me. She is wearing a red and orange sari. It is rare to see Indians running, particularly women. I like the way her gold bracelets jangle and the self-conscious look on her face as she runs. I smile. She catches my smile, grins back at me, but keeps running. Two people on the same road at the same time. Our lives meet, but in opposite directions and then we pass out of each other's life for ever.

Noon

"And it never failed that during the dry years the
people forgot about the rich years, and during the
wet years they lost all memory of the dry years. It was
always that way."

The sun is at its highest point. I am at my lowest. I walked and walked until now I just have to stop. My clothes arc soaked with sweat. A prickly heat rash rages round my waist, across my shoulders, through my armpits and round my heels. It stings and it itches, but only when I think about it. The difficult task is to relax the mind when it is twisted and angry and summon up the grace to accept with serenity the things that cannot be changed. Succeed at that and the itching fades fast.

I'm tired. Ferocious heat. Thirsty. Force myself to drink warm, chemical-flavoured water. Eyelids so heavy. Want to lie down and sleep. Ten minutes, an hour. It doesn't matter: there are more hours in this day than I can walk. At home, time is precious. Out here, I have cut everything unimportant so I have bought back time. I have as much of it as I need.

I'm irritable, impatient, out of love with India. Walking immerses me so deep that at times I feel I am drowning in it all, in the India described so well by Naipaul, "the broken roads and footpaths, the brown gasoline-and-kerosene haze adding an extra sting to the fierce sunlight, mixing with the street dust and coating the skin with grit and grime; the day-long cicada-like screech, rising and falling, of the horns of the world's shabbiest buses and motorcars."

I'm on the outskirts of a village. Pink bougainvillea flowers form tangled arches over people's doorways. I peel off my clammy shirt, remove my shoes and socks and flop into the shade of a bus shelter. The floor is covered in litter, broken glass, tobacco spit and peanut shells. I don't care. I sit cross-legged to keep the pressure off the soles of my feet. They feel as though they are on fire. Sweat pools in my Adam's apple. Mid-day, middle of the journey, mid life crisis: hell, it's been hard to get this far. Looking back, I feel I have done so little. So much remains to be done. Looking ahead down the road it is hard to convince myself to keep going, that things won't always be this hard. But I cannot give in: I'm committed to the day now and this filthy bus shelter is no place to call The End. I can't give in, but nor do I think I can make it to the end.

A very poor couple approach. I suspect they are homeless. Their movements are slow. They sit down next to me without speaking. They are sitting time away. The old man has a long beard and matted white hair. The lady is as fragile as a bird, old and hunched with empty eyes. Their clothes are faded. They chew *paan*[6], a mild narcotic. Their few remaining teeth are stained red. They spit continuously, a stream of red saliva splashing at my feet. It's too hot to care. I'm broken.

The old woman attempts to beg from me. It is the first time this has happened. She holds out her empty hand and gestures with her cloudy eyes. It is hard to see such poverty. But it is also alarmingly easy to ignore. What would happen if I gave her a

6 Betel leaf with areca nut and slaked lime paste.

hundred pounds? What impact would it have on this couple? It wouldn't really be a big deal for me. I can earn another hundred quid sometime. But I don't do it. I don't even summon the energy to smile politely. I turn my eyes and look away.

In the distance an engine ticks over. I hear a sweeping broom and the rattle of a water pump. These small sounds accentuate the quietness. The three of us sit in silence. I wonder what they are thinking. The lady rubs her husband's back, tenderly. She stands and walks slowly away down the road. A while later she returns, carrying a cup of *chai* given by a kinder soul than me. She hands it to her husband. And he takes the cup, and drinks. She sits back on her haunches. Not a word has been spoken. My life, my walk feels stupid.

I summon the resolve to continue and lift my bag back up onto my shoulders. The heat thumps me as I step out from the shade. I smile at the elderly couple. I'm light-headed, tired and weak. They smile back at me. I walk on.

Religion

"I have no bent towards gods. But I have a new love for that glittering instrument, the human soul."

Religion is an integral part of India. Even my river is a goddess, revered at shrines along her course. Pilgrims come from all over to bathe in her sacred waters.

Every day I walk past temples, churches and mosques. I share the road with *sadhus*, wandering holy men. We walk side by side in amiable silence. I pass men dressed as gods (perhaps gods dressed as men too). Buses and cars are decorated with favoured deities, often the elephant-headed Ganesh. Roadside shrines depict lurid scenes from the Vedas.

I encounter so many festivals, ceremonies and wedding parades. There are celebrations of gods and goddesses and boisterous village trumpet bands practising for their celebrations of gods and goddesses. Flowers are scattered, garlands of marigolds draped round necks and girls tie fragrant white jasmine into their shining black hair. There is music, always music, with men thumping drums enthusiastically to the excited skirling of pipes.

Market stalls often cluster at the entrance to the village temple complex, the hub of community life. I pause to buy bananas. There is an enormous trench fire outside the temple, its pulsating heat stronger even than the sun. The air shimmers. Music blasts from crackling speakers. Suddenly about fifty singing and dancing children appear down the street. They are wet and muddy and are holding leafy branches in each hand. On the command of chaperoning adults, who pretend to beat them with sticks, the children stop, prostrate themselves, then stand again and continue dancing forward. They dance past me, into the temple, and are gone. The music stops. As so often happens I have no idea what I just saw. Nobody speaks enough English to be able to enlighten me. If I travel completely unprepared, I must accept that the price of surprised delight is occasional bemusement.

I stop at a mosque. The *imam* is rocking back and forth in the doorway, quietly reciting the Koran with three young pupils. He breaks off the class to chat and asks me to take his photo. Then, to my surprise, he whips out an iPhone and takes my photo. He enjoys having the modern gadget whilst the foreigner just has a clunky, old-fashioned camera. Even his beard is more impressive than mine. The *imam* gestures at the mosque and explains that it is very old,

"The mosque is 200 years old; three generations. My phone is 3G and my mosque is 3G!"

I happen across a Christian ashram and am invited to a service. The chapel is in a wood beside the river. It is plainly furnished. The congregation of about twenty people are squashed together on wooden benches. On the altar is a wooden cross and a bronze dish of fire. The priest sits cross-legged on the floor. His orange robes are vivid in the narrow strip of sunlight from the door, left ajar to allow a slight breeze.

I listen to the birds singing outside. The ashram is a good place for sedately, serenely looking for yourself whilst at peace. I am sun-fried, half asleep and half entranced as the chants, candle light, incense and gentle goodness wash over me. But I will be on my way shortly. I look for myself by hurtling, hurting and sweating.

I understand snatches of the service as the priest jumps around between languages. He intones words I recall from my childhood church visits,

"...through ignorance, through weakness, through our own deliberate fault...

He raises a chapatti scarred in baking with the sign of the cross. It is comforting and familiar, even if I dislike the dogma.

...hear our prayer...

I think of all the tiny chapels across the world where this ritual takes place. The world is so vast. Instead of chasing to touch it all, perhaps I should just try to find the essence of it in one place, like the tiny space at the heart of the lotus flower in which, they say, lies all the universe: the moons, the stars, everything.

...he broke bread and gave it to his disciples, saying: take, eat...

Maybe I should try to make the most of my life by remaining at the centre, where I am right now, and living well here. Perhaps I don't need to be always yearning for the open road.

...for ever and ever, Amen."

Though I am not allowed in the inner sanctuary, I am welcome to visit the small Hindu temples in each village. I leave my shoes at the temple entrance with a shrivelled old lady and enter. The only sound is the pad of my bare feet. The central courtyard, its flagstone floor cool in the shade, is an oasis of calm, a break from the noise and bustle outside. Inside the temple is an elephant. Worshippers put coins in its trunk. In response, the elephant pats them gently on the head, then drops the coin into its master's hand.

Chipmunks race, tails up, around the elaborate pyramid above me. Monkeys watch from a wall. Swifts swirl across the sky, slipping the surly bonds of Earth. A man tosses a chunk of coconut towards a monkey. The monkey grabs it greedily and holds it tight to its chest. The man shyly offers me a piece too, then walks away. It tastes good.

A teenage girl, her hair in two neat plaits, with a garland of flowers round her neck and a school satchel on her back, pauses before a small carving of a god. Two candles flicker at its base. She puts down her satchel and squeezes her hands together in prayer. She is not at all self-conscious. The girl prays her concerns to her god, bends to pick up her satchel and then continues her walk to school.

A breath of breeze brings a scent of flowers. I treasure India's endearing love of flowers. I love India. I love this journey. If I have a daughter one day, I will call her Jasmine, I decide. But no, these are *my* scented memories, my time. She must be free to choose her own life, her own flowers and memories.

PILGRIMAGE

"We are the Pilgrims, master; we shall go
Always a little further: it may be
Beyond the last blue mountain barred with snow,
Across that angry or that glimmering sea."

Pilgrimage makes prayers come true. Or, to an unbeliever like me, a pilgrimage is about commitment and hard work, about the time invested and the time to think. These are the steps necessary to make most prayers and wishes come true.

Walking is both slow and difficult so it makes for powerful thinking time. Slow is good. With slowness and effort comes anticipation and clarity. Rewards have to be earned; ideas can be mulled over. I can appreciate the motivation of the pilgrims to Mount Kailash who prostrate themselves with each stride.

Ablaze in golden robes, hundreds of jovial pilgrims are marching down the road to their holy site with flags and banners. I smile as I pass amongst them. It is chaotic and spellbinding. Lazier pilgrims ride pillion on motorbike, their outfits streaming splendidly behind them. To the right is my river. Wheat fields stretch to my left. Villagers have spread wheat across the road to be threshed by the wheels of passing traffic.

Penance; redemption through suffering; searching – there seems to be an element of secular pilgrimage to my wandering, though that is not intentional. My walk does feel almost monastic and ascetic at times. I share the road for an hour or two with the turbanned, vermillion pilgrims. Eventually our routes diverge. They turn from my path at a junction in a road. I am sorry to see them go. I look down their road as far as I can, then take the other, the road that parallels the river. I am alone once again on my own forty days and forty nights in the wild. I am eating simply, living slow and testing myself out in the world. I do not know where the road is going. It doesn't matter. Wherever the river goes is the right way for me.

QUEST

"If one were properly to perform a difficult and subtle act, he should first inspect the end to be achieved and then, once he had accepted the end as desirable, he should forget it completely and concentrate solely on the means."

When I am on a journey, I know exactly where I am and where I am going. It is a lucid break from the muddy waters of day-to-day life. I miss some parts of my normal life violently when I am away; my wife, comfortable familiarity, warm beds and cold beers. I often wonder whether it is worth it. But I also know that without adventure I find myself drifting. I don't even treasure the things I miss when I am away. Another OK-but-not-great week. Another nice-but-not-memorable weekend. Not long until Christmas, to my next birthday, to my 40th, my 50th, retirement...

Time races on and I want to fill it with purpose. I want to keep the fire in my belly burning and to fall into bed each night satisfied that I have used my day well. This is why the feeling of being on a quest is an important aspect of my walk. Each day I am working hard towards an objective. That it is a relatively distant one can be demoralising, though it makes the eventual attainment more rewarding. A little time alone, afraid or forlorn is a worthwhile price to pay for feeling stronger, smarter and more alive.

Seeing it as a quest is perhaps grandiloquent. But the essence is the same whether it is a small journey like mine or the Odyssey. I'm taking a difficult journey and facing obstacles and doubt, in search of a goal. It ticks all the boxes of a quest.

The benchmarks for success and failure are clear. If I fail it will be my fault: because I am mentally or physically weak or because I am insufficiently brave. This will be painful but important to acknowledge in myself. Out here there can be no excuses, no sly shifting of blame. I have nobody to hide behind. There is no scaffolding of supporters propping me up. But I would rather attempt something difficult and glorious and then fail it than to merely trundle safely but tepidly onwards on life's ordinary course. And, if I do succeed in the quest then that will be down to me as well. I will feel proud and more self-confident. Committing to something difficult is like stepping into a furnace, to blaze brightly and to emerge forged hard into someone distinct. It may not necessarily make me a better person, but it does sharpen my focus on who and what I am.

Before I ever really explored the world and stretched myself, I was pleasantly content. But each adventure seems only to stoke the virus of restlessness and agitate the demons. Perhaps then to taste the fruit was folly. Each trip may add to who I am, but it also fuels more ambition. It never takes long before I find myself reaching for my globe, hatching the next project. If there is one thing the quests have not yet provided it is an enduring feeling of completion.

Perhaps this time things will be different I think, as I walk on. Perhaps I will return home after this walk, after all this seeking and striving, satisfied at last.

AFTERNOON

*"I have always lived violently, drunk hugely, eaten too
much or not at all, slept around the clock or missed
two nights of sleeping, worked too hard and too long in
glory or slobbed for a time in utter laziness. I've lifted,
pulled, chopped, climbed, made love with joy and taken
my hangovers as a consequence, not as a punishment."*

Brown grass and scrubby bush have replaced the lush fields and
palm trees. It reminds me of central Mozambique. I'm annoyed
at myself for thinking that. Why can't I just enjoy here as here?
Too many places remind me of other places, other days on the
road. My shadow marches along beside me. The way it mimics
my every move irritates me. I'm grumpy. I prefer life when I
have no shadow. It means there is no sun.

A hot wind is blowing. I'm struggling. I have stiff legs, bruised
feet and I am tired. I'm making no progress at all. I'm a hamster
on its stupid wheel. The damn road unrolls shimmering towards
the horizon. How many roads must I walk down? I can feel the
heat of the road through the soles of my shoes. Through my
soul. My feet are on fire. I feel every pebble, every step. I stop,
sit, remove my shoes. The soles have worn thin after hundreds
of miles of pounding. I squeeze my feet, gently. I wince. They
are badly bruised. I scour the roadside rubbish for something

to pad them with. At last, here is a positive side to the litter strewn across India. I find a car's inner tube, place my foot on the rubber and draw round it. I use my tiny penknife to cut an extra layer of inner sole. Every action is accompanied by a running commentary I do not understand from the inevitable gathering of people who crowd round me. My feet still hurt, but the new insole is an improvement.

A bridge spanning the river is not yet completed so people have to wade across to reach the other side. It's odd how the mind works: my first thought, as I see all these lightly-dressed Indians crossing the warm river beneath fluffy clouds, is a memory of attempting to cross a frozen river in a Siberian winter, following similarly in locals' footsteps. I was terrified of crashing through the ice into the death black water beneath. The kaleidoscope of strange mental link-ups is fascinating. But once I have negotiated my way across an unbridged river thousands of miles from home, the next time is understandably less of a surprise, less of an adventure. Perhaps I do not need to continually seek new places. Have I seen enough? Maybe there is a time to stop after all.

I shove my shoes into my rucksack and begin wading through the thigh-deep water. The current is gentle, the water warm and tiny shiny fish flash round my feet. There are a number of us crossing the river and we exchange smiles at how silly we all look.

The red dirt road on the other side heads slightly away from the river. The road is narrow and deserted. Farmers cajole oxen across tiny fields, dragging wooden ploughs. My trousers dry in minutes as I walk along. The silence is welcome. It wraps me in peace and I only want to curl up and fall asleep for all time. I know I need to eat. I am almost out of energy. I only manage about a mile before I have to lie down under a tree. I fall asleep until biting ants wake me. A stream of them run up my leg and into my pocket, eating my biscuits. The ants rush over my hands, biting, biting as I leap up and empty my pockets. I brush most of the ants off the biscuits – they are all the food I have left – and force myself to eat them. I know well the symptoms of heat exhaustion and I am being nailed by it now.

Even after all these miles on foot I still have a cyclist's mentality that considers 10, 20 or 30 miles to be not very far. On foot, smashed by the sun and by hundreds of miles of walking, today's final miles take many brutal hours.

I pass a wall on which is written, "Come unto me, all ye that labour and are heavy laden and I will give you rest." The gate is padlocked shut. I smile wryly and walk on, fuelled by obstinacy. I am light headed and nauseous, close to passing out. I suck the last of the unrefreshing, hot water in my bottles and stumble on towards the next well. I toss the metal bucket down into the dark well. It takes all my strength to haul it back up again. Green and stinking, the water is foul. The well has been contaminated by animal muck and rubbish. I take the water anyway and douse it with iodine.

The afternoon feels like an eternity. A motorbike stops and offers me a lift. I decline. Then another one does. I am so tempted. I consider cheating. Nobody would know. Just one small little ride. Just this once. Nobody would care. I think about doing the rest of the journey by public transport. It feels easy to justify...

This is it. This is the pivotal moment. In climbing speak

it is the "crux", the tiny section on which everything hinges. Get through this afternoon and I can get through anything. Capitulate now and it is all over. The rest of the journey would become irrelevant. Adventures like this depend on their "purity", however artificial and contrived that is. It may mean no supplemental oxygen when climbing a mountain, no re-supplies of food in the polar regions. Here it means no lifts: I am walking across India and therefore I must walk every step of the way from one sea to the next. This moment will define the trip. Not only will it determine this trip, I suspect it will determine my future. Can I still do it? Or do I no longer care enough? Have I had enough? I wish I was at home.

I keep walking. The arguments continue to bounce round my head ("keep going, stop, keep going..."), but I am still moving. One foot in front of the other. Westwards towards the sunset, towards the end, towards home.

The land is empty now. The road angles steadily upwards. There are no houses, no farmland, not even any litter. Monkeys scamper around rocky outcrops as I start to climb the mountain. Even through my fog of self-pity, I appreciate that this is a wonderful place. Wonderful except that I am almost out of water and it seems unlikely I will find any for some time.

Mountains do not care how I fare on their slopes. They were around for millions of years before my petty quest began, and they'll still be standing, beautiful yet uncaring, when my grandchildren's grandchildren feel the same call to test themselves. I'm pitting my guts and my luck against them. I might win or I might lose, my face marred by dust and sweat.

But they won't care either way. Perhaps that is part of the appeal of taking on challenges in wild landscapes. Do it for the doing, not for the praise of others. And don't be put off trying something big by the fear of failure and the sneers of people who have not done anything.

I glimpse more hairpin bends winding above me. As my craving for water escalates, the wind in the trees sounds like water. It is all-consuming to be desperately thirsty. I am nothing but a metronome now, bullying myself to keep going, step after step, hairpin after hairpin. I hate this walk. I am angry with myself for being here, for attempting this stupid challenge. How many more times must I put myself through this? This is ridiculous. Pointless.

Ridiculous and pointless, perhaps, but I do not give up. I came here for a battle. I am going to grit my teeth and get through.

And, although I still feel terrible – as bad as I have ever felt – I feel a tiny speck of pride in persevering. As I push through these final terrible hours, the sun is imperceptibly softening and sinking. It is easing off the pressure and filling the world with golden light. I have passed the test. I have almost earned my reward.

CHALLENGE

"You're too young a man to be panning memories,
Adam. You should be getting yourself some new ones, so
that the mining will be richer when you come to age."

Doing something fun is fun. There is plenty of space in life for
it. But fun is not going to shape me. It won't forge my direction
in life or remain seared in my memory down all the years to
come. The momentous moments in life are not merely fun.
This is where the appeal of challenging myself comes in. It is
what gives me my sense of identity.

A sceptical friend once described my masochism as "banging
your head against a brick wall to enjoy stopping." There is, I
admit, truth in that. There is a warm glow of contentment when
it is all over. But there is more to it. It is difficult to predict what
challenges I will need to overcome during a day on the road.
But I need to have the self-confidence to believe that I will be
able to cope, or that I will muddle through. Or at least that I
will be able to cope with the unpredictable consequences of not
being able to cope with the unpredictable situation.

Each time I succeed at something I thought would be difficult
I expand my boundaries and horizons a fraction. I am pleased to
have succeeded. It fires my ambition. I want that feeling again.
I set another challenge, daring myself to try things difficult and

rewarding with my diminishing days and strength. It's a vicious cycle familiar to all addicts: to get the buzz back you have to take a bit more, or take something stronger. My hope is that this is curable (the eternal delusion of the addict?) and that one day I will feel that I have done enough, that I have scratched the itch.

As well as striving for achievement and retrospectively relishing hard times, challenges help me to prove myself to myself. Overcoming something difficult is good for my self-confidence. I like fighting my weakness, laziness and nervousness in order to surprise myself and feel proud at what I have done. I store these experiences away in my memory to help me at some point in the future. Each one makes future challenges more attainable.

There is an element of using challenges to prove myself to other people too, either to win their praise, or as a metaphorical two-fingers to negative people. The "F***-You-Factor" is not the most noble of motives. But it is certainly effective. Thankfully, the older I become the less it features.

When thinking about which aspects of motivation to write about, I spoke to a fellow adventurer. An affable, humble man, he still confessed that earning bragging rights was an important part of why he did it all. The buzz of telling big yarns in the pub. To my surprise, for I am a secretly vain man, this aspect has never driven me. Perhaps I try to show off through my books (though I hope not). But I hate talking about what I do in pubs or at parties. I tell strangers I'm a teacher. I am proud that some of the most interesting things I have ever done remain unknown to virtually everyone else. There are no photographs of my journeys in my study. I don't buy souvenirs. The memories are not terrifically important to me. It is the thought of what comes next that drives me, not sitting back trying to recapture the glory.

At university I developed two fascinations: travelling the world and taking on physical challenges. I joined the Territorial Army to earn money to fund my adventures. The TA taught me to move fast, travel light and live efficiently. I took the first steps towards an education in "hardness". Being fit is easy, the saying goes. It's being hard that is hard. I learned to be tough on myself and set high standards, discovering that the benefits would spill over into all facets of life.

Small incidents stand out to me now. They often did not seem special at the time in the torrent of experiences that rush past us every day. But one by one they set me down the road towards this hot, lonely one I am walking today. Which moment to choose... Perhaps this one: we were on a coach one Friday night, driving to some grim training base somewhere in Scotland. It was probably raining. There would have been Irn-Bru. The Regimental Sergeant Major, who terrified me, came down the bus to chat to a group of us. He was an impressive man, ex Special Forces. He intimidated me, but I had huge respect for him.

He asked us about our plans after university. I had no idea. Everyone else spoke of joining the Army or jobs in the City. Sensible jobs. Ambitious careers. My turn came. My mouth opened. Mr Smart Arse.

"I'm going to be an adventurer."

My pals burst out laughing at my daft audacity. The RSM looked at me. He was not laughing. He stared hard at me. I braved myself to hold his stare.

"That's the best f****** answer I've heard all day."

After university, most of my friends joined the Army. I jumped on my bike and cycled round the world instead. But there was sufficient appeal in the Army to draw me back when I returned home.

I found myself, one cold morning, running the torture of a "bleep test" with other hopefuls at Regent's Park Barracks. I won. Last man standing. I beat a motley crew of strong men, far harder than me. How did I win? Doing eight hours of exercise a day for four years helped. But so too did four years of listening to my body, learning that pain would pass but the satisfaction of accomplishment would remain.

As we ran up and down I knew we were all hurting. All I had to do was refuse to stop. The theory is easy. The reality also becomes quite easy once it is habituated. Keep running until nobody else is willing to keep running. I'll never be the fastest but I'll never stop. Winner takes all. Who perseveres wins.

Unfortunately the Army messed up the date of my medical. I had to wait six months before I could continue, by which time life had moved on and the Army no longer fitted. So I never progressed much further than that bleep test. I suspect that the disappointment will always linger. Why? Because it was quantifiable. It was a chance to measure myself against set standards and other competent people. The problem with what my challenges, out there by myself, is that they are not quantifiable. Was I up to that course? I believe so. "Believe so" doesn't count. I will never know.

STRUGGLE

*"You can boast about anything if it's all you have.
Maybe the less you have, the more you are required
to boast."*

It's hard to get my head round the idea of a "struggle" whilst sitting in a comfy chair drinking tea and eating biscuits (and typing with o n e f i n g e r). But out there it makes sense.

I hate the gag reflex stench of road kill, the stickiness of sweat. I hate being stared at. I hate being asked the same questions a hundred times a day. But brutal days will end, as they always have and will continue to do. A different sunset, a different resting point, a different perspective. A little less road waits for me tomorrow. A little more road lies behind me. It's just as it always was. And I have come far enough now to begin brewing the bittersweet, cathartic feeling that comes with completing a hard task. Pride, surprise and relief.

People keep advising me to take the bus or offering rides on their motorbikes. I decline one offer, saying that I have just 15 kilometres to walk before the next village.

"15 kilometres?" replies the motorcyclist. "Oh, but the pain! Your legs..." And his head wobbles in horror.

Indians have no notion of the all-or-nothing aspect to my walk. Take one lift and the whole thing is futile. Even on the rare occasions when people understand that I am walking across India they will still say, "But I will just drop you at the next town. It is too far and too hot for walking."

I ask for directions. A man with a large moustache, hairy ears and thick glasses gives two options. I push him for clarification. "They are both exactly the same," he reassures me, noticing my concern at his vagueness. "One is 25 kilometres, one is 40 kilometres. No big difference. No problem." Experience has taught me that people have great difficulty giving directions to places they visit every day, if they only ever drive there.

Anyone scoffing at an extra 15 kilometres has clearly not done much walking. I take the shorter route. It would be silly masochism not to. But I walk it. Why don't I take a bus? It would be silly masochism not to...

Is it as simplistic as seeking pain? Why drive when I could walk? For the struggle. So why walk when I could crawl? "Seek pain, pain, pain!" cried Rumi. What are the rules? Where are the arbitrary boundaries in this search for a difficult life? They move and shift like sandbars. I'm not sure they stand up to rational scrutiny. I suppose they are defined by what feels right at the time, to me and me alone.

I want it to be hard. I want to spend most of the time dearly wishing I was not here, battling in my mind against excuses to stop. I derive a grim satisfaction from it, like sucking a lemon if you are desperately thirsty. I enjoy sticking through things that most people would not or could not endure. "You've got it in the neck – stick it, stick it – you've got it in the neck," repeated Captain Scott over and over on his way to the South Pole, a mantra for a struggle.

Some of the attraction is retrospective, the rose-tinted memories of completing something difficult. I look back at roads I've pushed myself down and I smile to myself. There was no applauding welcome at the end of those quiet roads, no tangible reward, no praise from others. The struggle reassures me I can still be hard. Or is "hard" the wrong word? Perhaps "daft"? But I would walk those roads even if I was not writing about them. It has to be for myself. It can only be for me, for we all have different thresholds of "difficult". Epic for me might be easy for you. It is my trial and my satisfaction afterwards.

Why do I value all this? Is it only to enjoy stopping? Perhaps it is to prove myself (in both meanings of the word)? To set me apart and boost my prestige because you can't do it, or won't do it? Because if I can do it, so can you? Because if I can do this I can do much more?

It is an old story, this one of redemption through suffering. From the Bible to King Lear and Crime and Punishment to our generation's contribution, I'm a Celebrity Get Me Out Of Here. Pre-dating all that is the colourful world of Hindu myth and ritual.

I hear it before I see it. Gunshots and drumbeats! I turn to see yet another religious procession. But even by India's high standards this one looks pretty mad. Dancing towards me are hundreds of men and women, draped with flowers and bearing large terracotta urns of burning wood on their heads. The fires light up the street. Sweat-wet drummers thrash out the rhythm for all to follow. A whirling, adolescent girl (a god, I am told) spins in a frenzy at the head of procession with crazed, unseeing eyes.

People urge me to join in. I am handed a blazing urn and I

dance down the road. Hot embers rain down. The atmosphere is charged. After a few mad minutes, I hand over my jar of fire and step back into the crowd. People are more interested in me than the event itself, which does not feel right. At the rear of the procession is a lorry, moving slowly behind the dancers. An effigy hangs from a gantry on the front. With a shock, I realise that it is a man hanging there. Suddenly I see that the man is hanging from hooks skewered through the flesh of his back, pulled tight by his body weight. He is conscious but motionless. I look into his eyes for some sort of clue to how he is feeling. His face is completely expressionless and his eyes are like the windows of an empty home. At his feet other devotees have 12-foot metal spikes rammed through their cheeks. They walk gingerly, bullying themselves to keep going, step after step.

The men look drained, almost ghoulish in their pain. I try to imagine how they feel. The humid air pulsates with drumming and wild energy and the glow of fire reflects in all our eyes. I think about the searing pain as the cold metal broke their skin. The dull, nauseating ache throughout the long procession. How long will they bear these wounds?

Why are they doing this? To prove something to themselves, to their loved ones, to their god. Because they will feel proud of their devotion and commitment long after the night's agony has subsided. No outsider can understand or share how these men feel, but that does not matter. Because, mad though their actions appear, this may be the greatest moment of their lives, a moment of lucidity and accomplishment far above anything they had ever imagined themselves capable of achieving. The moment that may define their life.

SUNSET

*"Better a thousand times that he should be a tramp,
and mend pots and pans by the wayside, and sleep
under trees, and see the dawn and the sunset every
day above a new horizon."*

Today may finish in so many different ways. This is wearing
and stressful over long periods but also enlivening. Today may
end in the home of kind strangers, motivated by sympathy and
curiosity to pluck me from the road saying, "come stay with us
tonight. Rest. Eat. And tell us your tale."

Day's end may be far from people's homes. The sun is setting. In
towns, people will be streaming home from work. But out here,
the road is empty. I am exhausted. It's time to stop. The hills
I slogged over are dark beneath a pink sky. Ducks fly quickly
overhead. I refill my bottles from a small stream. I don't have
a tent, but the sky is clear and warm. I find a flat spot to sleep
under a tree on the edge of a harvested field.

I light a small fire to cook rice. My dinner is just rice. It
means I only have to carry rice and a little pan. And it appeals to
the ascetic minimalism that is important to me on this journey.
I settle back against the tree and eat my rice.

Or my day may end walking into a town to find somewhere to sleep after the punishment of the afternoon. Under a radiant pink sky, a cricket match is in progress on the stubble of a harvested field. The bicycles of the players and spectators stand propped by the road. The pitch is pounded earth, the bowling fast and venomous. The batsman swings a big slog and cracks the ball high into the sky. Everyone shouts "Caaaatch!" and the poor fielder drops it. I smile in sympathy as I walk by.

Arriving in the town, I sit by the river to watch the last of the sunset. What a day. I am exhausted. Just another day. I stare towards the sun, along my river flowing with a golden blaze of sunlight. Towards all that I will discover tomorrow on the road. And I realise that I did not come to India for anything as simple and lovely as this wonderful scene. I came here for other things. This is merely a bonus. I feel a surprisingly large sense of satisfaction. This is my lucky day.

FREEDOM

"But the word timshel – "thou mayest" – that gives a choice. It might be the most important word in the world. That says the way is open... Why, that makes a man great... He can choose his course and fight it through and win."

How often do you wake in the morning with no idea where you will sleep that night? It is a hard way to live but sooner or later I miss it when I am not doing it. It is a declaration of independence. We hold these truths to be self-evident...

If you travel on foot then yours is the Earth, and everything that's in it. You need very little money. And you can go anywhere. All you need is the time and the pluck. And fear not, my friend, the darkness is gentler than you think. If nobody has seen you tiptoe into a field or a wood, then you are absolutely safe from harm. The night is a vagabond's ticket to sleep for free beneath the stars virtually wherever the fancy takes.

Many of my happiest nights have involved sleeping wild. A canopy of stars or a bright full moon, sleeping beside a campfire or swimming in a dark river: these experiences add to my life in a way that hotels or a sensible home can never match. Reduce my life to a small bag and my speed to walking speed and I feel as though I have everything I need in life.

The longest summer of my life was after I left school and needed to earn enough money to buy my freedom. So often in the world I have met people with fire in their bellies and questions on their lips who will never have the opportunity to see the world as I have. Raising the money for a plane ticket or getting a useful passport is out of the question. They will never be able to buy their freedom. But I could buy my freedom. I did so by trading minutes of my life for money in a mindless job. At last, I bought a plane ticket to Africa and the beginning of my life.

I stared, captivated out of the window for hours as the pick-up truck drove north from the airport towards the village that was to be my home for a year. The sky was enormous and blue. The land was flat and red and the black empty road ran straight towards the horizon. The air was hotter than I had ever known. A wild squeeze of incredulous excitement rose through me. I was in Africa. I really was in Africa! I was hooked.

Years have passed since that first adventure. I had no idea back then what lay in store for me down that long, straight road. But nor do I know today what lies in store for me down this long, straight road. Perhaps it is this unknown element and freedom of choice that is the key to the addiction that keeps me coming back for more.

Life on the road is a strange mix of paradoxes. I am free but I am a prisoner. I am a prisoner but I am free. I hate it and I love it. My days are routine and yet I cannot predict what may come along. I am free to turn left or right at the next fork in the road. It does not matter which I choose. Only that the choice may change the whole of my life. I appreciate how lucky I am to have that choice. It is certainly a privilege, a pressure and a responsibility.

NIGHTFALL

"When I was very young and the urge to be someplace else was on me, I was assured by mature people that maturity would cure this itch... I don't improve; in further words, once a bum always a bum. I fear the disease is incurable."

This single day on the road is just an ordinary day from any journey like this. Today struts and frets his hour upon the stage and then is heard no more. Tomorrow and tomorrow I will do it all again. Except that I will not do it again. I will do it for the very first time. Because every day on the road is new.

The sun has set across India. How will my day on the road end?

I watch the sun set. The entire sunset. Back home I am often too obsessed with being busy-at-all-times to just sit and stare. I'm so tired that I can't wait to sleep, even though it is early. I have turned feral, returning to the wild to live by the rhythms of the sun and the moon. I rig my mosquito net beneath the small tree. A gust of wind twitches the tree and my heart jumps. I have slept in hundreds of fields like this, so I am relaxed. But I am still alert for danger. I unroll my sleeping bag liner, plump up my rucksack to serve as a pillow and then lie down to sleep. I am cramped beneath the mosquito net. I am uncomfortable, sweaty and still hungry after my unappetizing pan of rice. But, after today, merely lying down in a field feels like a reward.

And what a reward! Above me are stars. More and more appear as my focus improves. The Milky Way too, and satellites and shooting stars. My wishes already came true. Far from streetlights and with neither my view nor my imagination enclosed by four walls and a roof, I am free to absorb the mind-blowing spectacle of the night sky. A moving, pulsing star that catches my eye turns out to be a firefly, flitting round above my head. You don't get those in a posh hotel. Walk hot miles with a pack on your back and you will sleep well. Live your day well, with enthusiasm, dedication and curiosity. Do this, and you will sleep well, even if you are lying in a corner of a foreign field far from home. I am so content lying here, having earned my sleep, that I try to force myself to stay awake to savour it. But I closed my eyes and I slept.

Nightfall in a dusty town is different again. People are bustling in and out of the temples, meeting friends or buying vegetables for dinner. I find a place to stay beside the bus station. It is cheap, dirty and identical to last night's. I dump my pack, swap the padlock on the door for my own and head out in search of food.

I walk the busy evening streets, alone amongst the strolling families and couples. I see sweet stalls, piled high and gleaming, sticky beneath hot bulbs. Jewellers are hunched over intricate repairs on their outdoor stalls. I see pots and pans, dusty sacks of dry red chillies, children's toys and snacks frying in broad cauldrons.

I see all this and know that the same story is playing out, right now, in tens of thousands of little towns all over India. I feel greedy for more. I want to see every town. I want to live every day in every town; every day that has ever been in every town. I want a satellite view from on high and a time machine to take me back and take me forward. And, at the same time, I want to burrow deep into every detail of right here, right now. I want everything. This is the intoxicating cocktail of wanderlust and the freedom to explore.

Take that man over there, the one staring blankly at me. He is sitting at a sewing machine outside a brightly lit shop, colourful with swathes of cloth. He has a moustache and is about 40 years old. That is all that I know about this man. A 40-year-old tailor perspiring in the hot Indian night. That is all you know about him too. But what stories he could tell us: stories unique in the history of mankind! Tales of a life growing up in India, a life so different to mine. His is just one out of a billion small stories here. But still, that is a one-in-a billion story. Surely that's a story worth hearing?

Butchers are packing away piles of unsold, plucked chickens from the tables they have been lying on all day, covered in flies and out in the sun. They will be put out for sale again tomorrow. They look revolting.

I enter a cheap-looking café. After such a hard day, I feel I have earned a delicious meal.

"What do you have to eat?" I ask, sitting down wearily.

"Chicken."

I arrive back at the lodge down the dark, rutted street. I hammer on the door. A single bulb outside the late night booze shop opposite is the only sign of life. The grumpy night watchman clears his throat and spits on the pavement as he lets me back in. The door to my room clicks closed behind me. I feel for the light switch. A pretty burst of blue sparks flash, the light flickers a few times then pings into life. Cockroaches speed to dark corners. The walls are covered with smears, stains and scuffs. I don't care. It's just the usual squalid, cheap room.

I am so tired. I undress. I pull off my trousers, the old nostalgic favourites, ripped on the right thigh and repaired with a bruise of purple cloth. I take off my shirt, the kind that looks smart in city offices. It is heavy with sweat and crusty with salt. I pull soggy, sweaty socks off my hot, aching feet.

I walk into the dirty bathroom. I look at my reflection in the small plastic mirror hanging from a nail. I pass my hand across the cropped stubble of my scalp. I look terrible. Almost broken. I grin. Almost.

Then, the day's reward: I scoop a jugful of water from a bucket on the floor and pour it over my head.

Bliss.

You will have your reward, so long as all you want is a bucket of water.

I set up my mosquito net and climb into bed. Outside, the clamour of India continues. Another day on the road is over. I answered the call. I am so content lying here, having earned my sleep, that I try to force myself to stay awake to savour it. But I closed my eyes and I slept.

~The End~

The Last Day: to the Source

"I know that it might be better for you to come out from under your might-have-beens, into the winds of the world."

"Beep... beepbeepbeepbeep... BEEPBEEPBEEPBEEP."

I know instantly where I am. It is a new day. India.

I feel fired with purpose. It is the last day.

I step over the sleeping night watchman and out of the dingy lodge. I start to walk. Really walk. I walk through the hilltop town past all the sweepers. I return the cheery greeting from the *chai* stall, its light bulb shining on the steam rising from hot drinks in this cold hilltop dawn. But today I decline their invitation. Today I have miles to go before I sleep. I want to walk 50 miles. To see if I can. To show that I can. Because I know I can.

I have already zigzagged down all the hairpins to the valley floor and climbed back up the far side by the time the first rays of sun burst over the horizon.

"Here comes the sun," I sing, for the last time, and I lengthen my stride right through the morning, through the fierce mid-day hours and on into the afternoon. I am so fit now, lean and hardened to these days on the road. And this is the last day, so I need keep nothing in reserve for tomorrow.

At the start of this walk, the people who lived along the river delta had no idea where their river had come from. Now, hundreds of miles later, high in these green hills, nobody knows where their river is busily rushing to. I have followed their river, my river, all the way, filling in the blanks. And now I am almost at the source.

Big, bright flowers bloom up the sides of the small houses. Forests sweep down the steep valley sides. I gaze at distant blue mountains and want to explore them all. It is a beautiful place.

I climb a sinuous rural road. The sky is darkening with storm clouds. They fill the sky like clods of earth. An angry headwind is brewing. I smell the storm first and then it hits me, its awesome power saturating me in seconds. People dash from the sudden rain under the eaves of buildings. They gesture urgently for me to join them.

"Come in!" they laugh, "We'll give you shelter from the storm."

But I am happy out here. I just wave and stride on. Clay-red streams rush down the road. I am as wet as it is possible to be. To thunder and sunshine I add wind and rain on my list of things that make me feel alive. The rain fizzes and bounces. I love it. Right, let's move!

I leave the road and continue up a small track through long grass and wet bushes. Leeches writhe on my ankles. My legs stream with blood. I don't care. They don't hurt. I can't feel them. And this is all about feeling.

Walking 50 miles in a day is an unimportant act. But it means a lot to me. It is one day that represents much of my adult life. Walking that far is stupid. It hurts. But it is not about the walk. That is only a metaphor for how I want to live. Years ago I began reading books about adventure and endurance. I devoured books of derring-do in far off lands. The books seemed so far beyond my own world that I read them purely as fun, fantasy books. But little by little, something sparked my curiosity. I began questioning myself, wondering whether some day I might be able to do anything like the things I was reading about.

Back then I could never have walked 50 miles in a day. No, that's not right: when I began this life I *would not have believed* that I could walk 50 miles in a day. Little by little I have changed until now I believe that it is possible to succeed at almost any big idea. Not much is required except the boldness to begin and the perseverance and initiative to keep moving. I am slowly rising towards the challenge of making the most of my potential. I have already exceeded what I once imagined my limits to be.

So, this is who I am now. I just need to work out who I will become. I think nervously about what lies ahead, about my future. Can blasting 50 miles through a rainstorm really prepare me for real life? For the last fifteen years my answer would have been, "Definitely!"

But now that I am about to put it to the test, I am not so confident. Am I ready? The question does not really matter: my future is racing towards me regardless of whether I am ready or not.

And so I reach the hilltop temple. The start of the river, the end of my walk. My walk and my river are distilled to this one small pool that I have walked so far to reach. Red hibiscus flowers float in the holy well. A priest blesses pilgrims. I am surprised how happy and emotional I feel. It has been a difficult, fascinating adventure. It is no era-defining epic, but it feels satisfying nonetheless. The priest dips a silver chalice into the well and draws a small draught of spring water. He pours it over a pilgrim's head and murmurs a prayer of gratitude to the river goddess. And so the water begins the journey I have just finished.

I give thanks to the river too, for guiding me through new experiences and for reminding me what I hold dear. I owe it to myself, whatever happens, to cling tight to those things. It is time to return to England. Life is going to be different this time.

Regardless of how my road unrolls in the future, this walk has reminded me what a life of adventure is really about. More than anything else, it is a state of mind. It is an attitude of curiosity, bold enthusiasm, ambition, effort and a rejection of mediocrity. I don't need to walk across India for that. I can find it anywhere, if I am only willing to chase it. I have the choice.

~The End~

The Last Day: to the Sea

"Each day looks as beautiful as the roads that lead to the sea."

"Beep... beepbeepbeepbeep... BEEPBEEPBEEPBEEP."

I know instantly where I am. It is a new day. India.

I feel fired with purpose. It is the last day. Though, of course, there is no such thing as a last day. To make an end is to make a beginning. The end – the source of the river – is where I start from. So, while the light fails on a winter's afternoon in England, I have crossed the watershed in India and am walking down to the sea. Downhill for the first time in India.

The quiet road curves away into the tall trees. I fill my water bottles from streams trickling down the steep slopes. I stoop and sink my head into the cold, gurgling underwater world. It is a blissful escape.

I lengthen my stride, through the morning, through the fierce mid-day hours and on into the afternoon. I have left the trees and hills behind now. I am on the coastal plain. I have left almost everything behind. The final few hours are ferociously hot. Approaching the end now, I force myself to slow down, to rest awhile, eat some food and savour it all. I want to enjoy the end. For this time it really does feel like the end.

Ahead of me, the sky is huge and empty. A sea sky. I pass beneath a final row of palm trees and out onto the beach. I have nothing left in reserve. I take off my pack and walk slowly down the soft sand into the sea. Ending a journey at an ocean is very satisfying. It feels definite. I can go no further. The beach stretches away in both directions, white, straight and washed clean to the high tide line. The heat has gone from the sun, but it still shines brightly on the water. And I stare out to sea, beyond the wooden fishing pirogues, and out to the horizon. And I wonder what lies on the other side.

—✿—

I feel absolutely drained and very content. It's just the beach, the sea and me. There is no end of adventure hype, no World Record to validate or sponsors' press release to issue. This is how I like it. I am alone except for one boy, aged about ten, with a red t-shirt and a crew cut. He comes and sits beside me on the sand. We have no common language so we just sit quietly. I like being able to share this moment with someone, even this silent little kid. The waves roll gently up the sand and the air smells of sea salt. This is a fine place to end a journey.

After some time the boy notices me watching the translucent crabs that scurry across the sand. He sets about trying to catch one for me. He darts after them, grabbing and missing, grabbing and missing. I watch and smile. The crabs bolt down holes as the waves slide in and out. He digs furiously at the wet sand.

Again and again he fails to catch a crab but we both enjoy sharing the futility of it. It is an endless task, an impossible task, but for that brief moment it is filled with purpose and pleasure. And that seems good enough for me.

The sun sets and the boy goes home. But I stay on the beach staring out to sea. The first stars begin to shine. The evening air is warm. So much has happened since I began chasing these journeys down the never-ending road. I haven't done all that I want to. But it feels good to at least be on my way. These are the best days of my life. Out here I am free. I know what I am doing. I am good at it. I am happy. I am really living.

It is dark now. And tears are streaming down my face. It is time to go. I can't keep escaping. I don't want to keep escaping. But I know that I will never live the life of my choice in quite the same carefree way again. Opening the box never made Pandora happy. But at least she had the guts to open it. These are selfish tears, yes. But they are also tears of happiness. I have finished this journey. I'm a lucky man. For now it is time to go home. Time for real life. Time to really live. I'm going home to become a father.

~The End~

ABOUT THE AUTHOR

Alastair Humphreys is an adventurer, author and blogger. He has cycled round the world, walked across southern India, sailed the Atlantic Ocean, crossed Iceland, run marathons through the Sahara desert and walked a lap of the M25. He is currently training for an expedition to the South Pole.

Alastair has written five books about his adventures. He is in demand as a motivational speaker, speaking worldwide at conferences, schools and events.

Alastair has been shortlisted as National Geographic's Adventurer of the Year.

www.alastairhumphreys.com

BY THE SAME AUTHOR

Moods Of Future Joys

Alastair Humphreys spent four years cycling round the world, crossing 60 countries and five continents. *Moods of Future Joys* is the story of the first remarkable stage of the expedition, from England to South Africa. It recounts an epic journey that succeeded through Humphreys' trust in the kindness of strangers, at a time where the interactions of our global community are more confused and troubled than ever.

With a foreword by Sir Ranulph Fiennes.

Thunder & Sunshine

Alastair Humphreys' ride of 46,000 miles was an old-fashioned adventure: long, lonely, low-budget and spontaneous. *Thunder & Sunshine* is the second part of the remarkable journey, covering the Americas and the ride back through Asia and Europe to finish his journey.

With a foreword by Bear Grylls.

Ten Lessons From The Road

Alastair Humphreys had time on the road to reflect why he was cycling round the world, what had motivated him to begin and how he hoped to use those lessons in the future. The lessons of the road.

Ten Lessons from the Road breaks those lessons into 10 simple chapters, illustrated with experiences from the journey and stunning photography that is sure to inspire and encourage.

The Boy Who Biked The World

Tom really wants to be an explorer.

His favourite book is an atlas. His schooldays are spent daydreaming about travelling from Tibet to Timbuktu. The more that people told him he couldn't cycle round the world, the more determined he became. Follow Tom's adventures through Africa in this first installment of a series of three books.

Tom's journey bears uncanny similarities to the author's own ride round the world...

All books are available, signed by the author, from
ww.alastairhumphreys.com

Your feedback on *There Are Other Rivers* would really be appreciated:
www.tiny.cc/amazon_book_review
www.twitter.com/al_humphreys [ThereAreOtherRivers]
www.facebook.com/alastairhumphreys
books@alastairhumphreys.com

Author, editor, proofreader, marketer, distributor and walker: Alastair
Humphreys. If the book is terrible there is only one person to blame.
Cover design by Jim Shannon (www.ngicreative.com)
Book design & typesetting by Helen Steer (www.sorryforthemess.com)
Printing by Absolute Proof (www.absoluteproof.co.uk)

There Are Other Rivers is available as an ordinary book, an eBook, a
Foldedsheet "mappazine", a book of photography, a PDF download
and an audio book.
For details see www.alastairhumphreys.com/ThereAreOtherRivers

Please consider donating this book to a charity shop once you have
finished with it.